Faith That Moves Mountains and Smashes Strongholds

Faith That Moves Mountains and Smashes Strongholds

Dr. R. G. Ellies

Wipf & Stock Publishers
Eugene, Oregon

FAITH THAT MOVES MOUNTAINS AND SMASHES STRONGHOLDS

Copyright © 2007 Dr. R. G. Ellies. All rights reserved. Except for brief quotations in critical publications or reviews, no part of this book may be reproduced in any manner without prior written permission from the publisher. Write: Permissions, Wipf & Stock Publishers, 199 W. 8th Ave., Suite 3, Eugene, OR 97401.

Wipf & Stock Publishers
199 W. 8th Ave., Suite 3
Eugene, OR 97401

ISBN 13: 978-1-55635-467-0

Manufactured in the U.S.A.

Contents

Acknowledgements	vii
Introduction	ix
Part One: What Exactly Is This Kind of Faith	1
Chapter 1: What's In a Word	3
Part Two: People Who Modeled True Faith	29
Chapter 2: Abraham, the Father of Our Faith	33
Chapter 3: Two Men with Death-Defying Faith: Enoch and Noah	40
Chapter 4: Caleb, a Gentile with an Ageless Faith	53
Chapter 5: Rahab, Gentile Grandparent of the Messiah	64
Chapter 6: Shadrach, Meshach, and Abednego: Faithful Men Aflame	71
Chapter 7: Job: Faith for When the Mountain Falls on You	81

Part Three Critical Issues of Mountain Moving Faith — 99

    Chapter 8: The Absolute Necessity of Faith — 103

    Chapter 9: Understanding Saving Faith — 114

    Chapter 10: The Difference between Faith Works and Faith Works — 133

    Chapter 11: Secret to Mountain Moving Faith: God's Faithfulness — 155

Acknowledgements

I wish to express my indebtedness to all members of staff and members generally of the New Jerusalem Ministries. How I love this church. It has been birthed through the exercise of the faith principles that this book speaks about. By faith, it has grown into a large, vibrant body of believers that now fellowship at three separate campus locations. I can only imagine how, by faith, this ministry will continue to grow, as it fulfills all that God intends for it to become.

My gratitude also must go to the diligent efforts of the Carty and Simmons families who served so faithfully by providing research assistance, manuscript proofreading and serving as my production assistants. Without you dear friends and brethren, this book would never read as it does.

I also wish to express my special thanks to two professors whose work and fellowship during the four years of my doctoral work, first to Dr. Dale Kietzman for so ably demonstrating the man of faith model, and second, I would like to especially thank Dr. James Krames, whose exegetical training has made the Word a most understandable document, and has equipped me to analyze the Word with such acumen that I can venture into this writing ministry.

I would also like to express my deep appreciation to my dear wife, whose patience with the long hours of study and writing kept me from her fellowship.

Also, permit me to express my praise to the precious Holy Spirit who so carefully guided me through the research, and the writing of this book.

Finally, I share with you, dear reader, that my prayer has been, and remains, that you will find this study of the subject of faith transformational—and many strongholds will crumble under the wielding of the faith this book encourages you to exercise.

Dr. Russel G. Ellies, Senior Pastor.

Introduction:
Faith that Moves Mountains and Smashes Strongholds

The subject of faith is rooted in God. It pervades and permeates every page of Scripture. It is as essential to the spiritual life of true believers as breath is to physical existence.

The Christian church possesses a rich repertory of literature on the subject of faith that is theologically sound, and intensely practical.

The purpose of this book is to help the believer, with the guidance of the Holy Spirit, to find a new passion for the Lord and a new desire to wield the gift of faith to change their families, congregations, and worlds. To this end we have adopted this theme, which is expressed above.

One can imagine that I venture into this subject with some serious misgivings, since I am attempting to deal with a subject that has been thoroughly explored. What, I think, I bring to the subject is an understanding of the subject that has emerged from the crucible of my own reflections, and has been the force for the ministry I have conducted for the past decades.

I bear testimony to learning to tap into the mighty working of the living God through the exercise of faith at a high level. It is this experience—almost a how-to—that I desire to share with the reader.

As I take up my pen, I am suddenly conscious of the unfathomable debt I owe to countless theologians and expositors whose love for the Word, and commitment to produce its content with a high level of accuracy. The only thing one can know about faith is what the Word declares about it.

I consider it a great privilege to use the exegetical skills that I gained in my doctoral work and Dissertation to present an understanding of faith and show how it works, at once with instantaneous results, while at other times, fulfilling its workings over a period of time, but always with God honoring, life blessing results.

Since you are eager to know how to tap into the fullness of God's mighty power—I dedicate these special insights to you.

Pastor Russell Ellies, D.Min

PART ONE:
Understanding Mountain Moving Faith

Chapter 1

What's In a Word?
Getting the Meaning of the Word FAITH Clearly in Mind

Introduction

On a day of destiny—June 8th, 1977 I became a man of faith. (As you read this book you will discover how.) While I had lived as a "man of straw", I gleefully embraced with steel-like strength my new life. I was determined to live by faith. During these past three decades, my desire to be a man of faith has only mushroomed.

Small wonder, then, that I have discovered its power and presence on every page of the Book from Genesis to Revelation. Every one of its authors heralds the many aspects of this vital truth, directing the human being, more so the believer in Christ, to view faith from a divine perspective. So what does the word faith actually mean?

It is my privilege to serve as your guide as we enter a realm of life insights as rich in meaning as the Promised Land was in material wealth, "flowing with milk and honey". Together, we will probe the concept of faith, first as a word to be clearly understood, then as a life changing force.

We will hear it spoken in the language of Abraham, and later as it emerged from the mouths of Jesus and the Apostles.

So, on this Jordan like moment before we embark into the experience of getting the benefits from this simple word, "faith", permit me to share with you how much I treasure the privilege of sharing this journey with you, knowing God, and how to use faith to access His blessings, has proven to be so personally and professionally rewarding, I am inclined to consider the above mentioned date (30 years ago) as my true birthday.

A Word about the Process

Getting an understanding sufficiently clear to enable you to apply it to many areas of your life is the purpose of any word study. Think of it like peeling an apple. To find out what it is really all about, you remove the stem, expose the skin, slice away the pulp, and uncover the seeds. Suddenly, your understanding of an apple is transformed into something on the level of a life enhancing thought "Wow, with a few of these little 'fellas', I could grow some trees to feed my family! I would never lack for snacks or desserts as long as I live."

By obtaining a clear understanding of the meaning of a word, fat with flavor, and delicious with meaning, you not only gain practical insights to use to bless your life, and, in many ways you get a pleasurable treat.

Ask any person of faith the meaning of the word faith, and you will get a variety of answers with the words, such as, *believe*, feel, and *think* in the sentences. But, for all of us, the idea of really having to come up with a concise, accurate, clear definition of the word, we all start running for the dictionary.

Our goal is not to spend our time together in the library. However, to show you by Biblical fact, and godly examples, how you can live so abundantly that no mountain or stronghold threatens your peace and safety. But, without a true understanding of the very word at the heart of this discussion, we might be wasting many valuable words.

So we begin, like surgeons to probe this wonderful word to get all the insight it can deliver.

What's In a Word?

X-Ray Analysis of What True Faith Is All About

John G. Paton, a revered missionary pioneer, was making a translation of the Bible into the language spoken in the country where he was a missionary and searched long and hard for a word for "Faith". The native entered his room and, tired out, flung himself down on one chair, resting his feet on another then remarked how good it was to "lean his whole weight on the chairs". Paton noted the word and it became his word for faith.

Nothing is more important than that we gain a clear understanding of the meaning of faith. We shall now seek to analyze the Biblical words that are translated "faith", and "believe", both in the Old Testament (as Hebrew) as well as the New Testament (Koine Greek).

Then we shall look at the way Jesus and Paul used the word, and draw some practical conclusions to help us to personally apply these insights to become people of faith.

My interest for faith stems, in part, from my desire to minister to your heart by guiding you to understand it and enjoy the rich life that it can facilitate; after so many years of counseling people, and dealing with "fuzzy thinking" about faith, my desire is to not just explain it but to also de-mystify it. I am convinced that it is essential to show how important and practical it is for Christian living, and to attempt to correct much misinformation about Biblical faith which I view as ineffectual and potentially dangerous. False teaching destroys faith by replacing it with a counterfeit faith that can warp our conception of God and His intentions toward us.

Part One: In a Word, the Meaning of Faith

Old Testament Roots of the Matter

Words matter. And first words really matter if one desires to gain a clear understanding of the meaning of a word. Let us first look at the Hebrew words for faith. They not only set the parameters of faith, they became the forebears of the Greek words we shall study.

The Hebrew words paint a picture that is very consistent with the nuances of meaning the Greek word enjoys. By beginning with the very word that Abraham used for faith, we will get information we can use in our investigation of its Greek equivalent, *pistos*.

Hebrew Word: AMAN אָמַן

I love the Hebrew language because it is the tongue of people who were not so much philosophical, but theological, and whose concepts about God and the life He called them to follow were very practical, almost tactile (instead of being abstract).

As a result, their word for faith is a word that speaks of this as a concrete concept, shaping the meaning we associate with faith into something so practical you feel you could find it in a toolbox. Let's get a close look at this word.

This word is derived from a root word, אָמַן,. This root word comes three concepts:
1. "Forearm"
   From this four ideas were conjoined:
   - The idea that this is the essential measurement of size and distance
   - The idea of a "mother-city" the place on which one rests when an infant;
   - The idea that this is the way one will view what is "out in front" since, in battle, men, stuck their forearms out in close hand-to-hand combat to protect themselves; and,
   - A foster-father, i.e., "nourisher". i.e. a male that assumes the role of caring for a very small child by supplying its food and everything else it requires for living during this state of vulnerability, including being fed from a bottle.

Think about the rich meaning of that Hebrew root? When you connect the essence of these ideas this incredible composite insight emerges: a person of faith is one whose every plan is measured by a confidence in the foster-father to supply every need.

2. "Mother-City"

A second concept imbedded in this root word: a "place": it is called "the mother-city", i.e., the capital city of one's existence. Add this piece of the puzzle and you see that it represents a way of life, where one "resides" by conducting all of one's life according to a worldview dominated by a realization that one's life is built around a relationship.

3. "Lifestyle"

A final concept, closely related to the second one, is the idea that this "place", (think of it as a virtual place), is where one lives with people who share the same lifestyle, the same roots, the same source of nourishment and strength, and who plan their lives individually and corporately according to the will of the One from whom it looks to as the source of its life.

From this root, one discovers, in the Old Testament, that the idea of faith was really not just an abstract concept, but a real, tangible way of living one's life as a people of a Covenant God. So, naturally, as the word evolved, it became known as the type of action or response one gives or lives by as a humanly response to the actions and will of their God, who had expressed His will in the Torah and other Scriptural writings.

All of this comes together in the writing of the Psalms, where the dedicated heart blends the concepts of faith (i.e., faith in the Living Lord) along with fear (i.e., fear of disobeying of displeasing Him). This special dynamic resulting from the tension created by living between these two concepts becomes the heart of the relationship of the person of faith in the later eras of the Old Testament. It becomes the attitude that governs a lifestyle of a person whose exclusive trust is in the Living God. This becomes evident in the way in which these shades of meaning appeared in the Greek word for faith, **pisteo**.

Check out the way the Old Testament words for *pistos*, i.e. faith, faithful, and belief were translated into Greek about 200 years before the birth of Jesus:

   a. `*Amun* "faithful" (Prov. 14:5; 20:6).
   b. `*Emunah* "faithfulness" (Dt. 32:4).
   c. `*Aman*: "be faithful, be firm" (Nm. 12:7; 1 Sm. 2:35; Is. 22:23).
   d. `*Aman,*: "something trustworthy" (Dn. 2:45-Aramaic).
   e. `*Emesh,* "truthful" (Prov. 14:25).
   f. *Yether,* "remainder, excellent" (Prv. 17:7).
   g. *Tsaddiq* (ζαδδίξ), "righteous" (Job. 17:9).

When they are assembled into a composite picture of the Old Testament meaning of faith" "(to believe") you get a very good understanding of what faith means: To exercise trust with total reliability, and trustworthiness to the point of excellence according the standard that God considers valid, i.e., righteous. The idea is supported by this metaphor, "solid like a rock".

The Psalmists wrote much about this, describing the LORD, and the people who trusted in Him as people whose trust was immutable. As it pertains to the LORD, His faith-keeping is tied to Him steadfastly keeping His covenants with those who trust Him such as with David (Ps. 89:28). At the same time, God chooses "faithful" men to execute His will such as Samuel (1 S. 2:35; 3:20). Nehemiah (9:8) said that this was the basis for God's love of Abraham, he possessed a "faithful" heart in his relationship with the Lord.

It also marked the other spiritual giants, e.g., Moses, Isaiah, Jeremiah, and many more Old Testament saints.

Abraham's Faith: An Excellent Example

When one studies the life of Abraham, one discovers this same concept born out in a living example. As Romans 4:13-22, declares, Abraham received the promise through righteousness, which he appropriated by faith. This, as Paul, here shows, involved transforming things, which are not, as though they were; and thereby bringing them into reality is nothing short of a miracle.

This was the secret of Abraham's faith. He believed God's testimony and looked for the performance of His promise, firmly hoping, even when the case seemed hopeless. And in this moment of weakness he learnt a great principle: such moments when we must rely totally upon the Lord; these are the very moments where we learn if our faith is real, or weak.

The proof of weak faith is that it will always search for backups, human means that it can look to for solution if all else fails. Why do men turn to such devices? They create such "add-ons" because they stagger at God's promises.

Because Abraham had discovered true faith, he entertained no fear of loss—because he considered a life without faith as the complete loss of his future. He also saw that by obeying God by offering Isaac he had an opportunity to honor God, as only great faith can. No wonder his encounter with God on Mt. Moriah resulted in the Lord imputing to him righteousness.

How sad that, today, the doctrine of faith does not receive the attention it deserves. Great emphasis is laid upon human conduct. A man's creed is said to be a matter of indifference. Yet a man's life is governed by what he believes (creed); and what he believes determines where that faith is focused. So the object of one's faith, i.e., creed, does matter.

In the next chapter I will investigate the life of Abraham more closely to gain more insights into the nature of true faith and how to use it to bring blessings to your life.

Derivative of Aman

With this basic understanding of the Hebrew word we, "*aman*", let's explore a word that it birthed, "*emuna*". This is the word that the Bible translated, variously, as "to be faithful"; "to be reliable"; and "to be steady".

By blending these shades of meaning with our root word, a very helpful insight emerges: "being true in one's trust of God, will make you a trustworthy person." How this flies in the face of an idea promoted by postmodernists, "It doesn't matter what you believe in just so you believe."

Can we really experience the work of the Holy Spirit if the object of our faith is not the Lord Jesus and the Word of God, but faith in faith? Such people are content to feel religious because they cannot accept the fact that absolute truth does exist, and find it and becoming loyal to its directions to the point of trustworthiness.

Thank God for the Scriptures, which teach us that God is truth, Faithful in all He does and says, and therefore worthy of our trust. Due to Adam's sin, we lost the ability to trust God, but in Christ, we not only receive faith as a gift, but we are taught, by the indwelling Spirit, how to use it to find the abundant life He desires for us. As a result of this concept, man not only knows how to become a true believer (repentance), but also how to live in a loving relationship (by faith).

As the prophet Habakkuk described this process, "…the just shall live by faith…" Because Abraham grasped this principle and embraced it, something extraordinary occurred in his life, which Paul describes this way: "Then he (Abraham) believed in the LORD; and He reckoned it to him as righteousness." Although Abraham did the believing, it was really God who caused the righteousness to be imputed or designated to Abraham's account. This is the root of righteousness by faith alone. (This is why postmodernism is wrong).

What made it work for Abraham will also make your life of faith so effective. He believed that God would provide a substitute. This side of Calvary, we know that this involved the Lord Jesus, who by His death, enabled the Father (who could never overlook sin not covered by the blood) to give the righteousness of the Son to anyone who places their trust in that Jesus as their Lord and Savior. We become part of Christ when we believe and trust Him. Our outlook becomes, like Isaiah's, "O LORD, Thou art my God; I will exalt Thee, I will give thanks to Thy name; for Thou hast worked wonders, plans formed long ago, with perfect faithfulness." *Isaiah 25:6*

What caused Isaiah to burst into such praise? He suddenly realized that he had reached this state of trusting relationship because God, in His faithfulness, had been working through Isaiah's past experiences to bring him to this ability to trust the Lord.

Notice this phrase, "perfect faithfulness", above. The Hebrew built it by placing two words for faith side by side. This combination suggests this truth, "In His faithfulness, God is faithful. i.e., there is no way any slight mark of unfaithfulness could be part of Him. He is ultimately faithful, His Word is sure and trustworthy".

So, with this new understanding of the Hebrew word for faith, *aman*", let us advance to the New Testament to examine how its Greek New Testament equivalent word for "faith", *pistos*. In doing so, we will discover even more insights between faith and faithfulness to help us to know how to move those mountains.

New Testament Word for Faith, Pistos

In checking every critical Greek-English Lexicon in my library, I was able to build a composite idea of the meaning of faith that mirrored the concept described in the Old Testament. To help you appreciate how I arrived at

What's In a Word?

this understanding of the meaning of *pistos*, consider these definitions offered by the dictionaries on my shelf:

- "the persuasion of the mind that a certain statement is true; primary idea is to convey trust; and that thing, being true, is therefore worthy of trust (Easton).
- Faith is a commitment by the human will and mind to the knowledge about the object of one's faith as being true.
- Faith is being convinced that Jesus has been raised from the dead; and thereby, becomes the Messiah and author of true salvation.
- Faith is not just the assent of the intellect to revealed truth; it is the practical submission of the entire man to the guidance and control of such truth, which distinguishes true faith with that the devils hold.
- Faith is the result of the work of the Holy Spirit.

As I investigated the Lexicons, I began to see a pattern: *Pistos*, in its various shades of meaning contains these reoccurring ideas: to be convinced to the point of possessing great confidence in the word of God, and to not just embraced their words as true and worthy of complete trust, but also to act upon them with such consistency that one becomes faithful to the One in whom your trust is placed.

Reflecting on all these lexicons, I was struck by the variety of actions they insisted that faith, as a verb involved, trusting, cherishing faith or trust; believing, full of faith, faithful; believing (in Christ), a (Christian) believer; believers when used as an active verb (where the subject is doing the action).

As a noun, *pistos*, becomes a defining quality; hence, those who believe in Jesus, enter a state that so defines them that they become "believers". As the concept of faith matured during the ministry of the apostles, and captured on paper in the Epistles, we see that the meaning of faith had matured into a full blown trust in the Lord Jesus that included these three main elements, mutually connected and requisite, though according to circumstances sometimes one and sometimes another may be more prominent:

1. Being absolutely confident about the trustworthiness of something/someone to the point that their words, or ideas, or assertions are elevated to the level of unimpeachable fact.

2. This high level of confidence resulted from having acted on the promise in a way that turned out to be true to the very conditions the promise laid out. Therefore, the promise, by acting upon it, proved itself to be totally trustworthy, therefore, worthy of your complete confidence, therefore, you willingly embrace it as fact and act upon it with total confidence.
3. Being fully convinced acknowledgement of the revelation of grace resulting in a self-surrendering fellowship (adhesion) to it; followed by acting with fully assured, unswerving trust (and with this at the same time hope) in the God of salvation or in Christ.

With the meaning of pistos nailed down, I venture to show you two important nuances of the meanings that will add to your understanding of what faith means.

Difference a Preposition Makes

Permit me to tackle this theological issue: what is the difference between believing in Jesus and believing on Jesus. You would not believe how many seminary term papers have been written on this subject. To keep it simple, permit me to tell you a story that illustrates the difference.

A university professor approached a pastor with this question. Pastor, since you are learning Greek, what is the difference between believing IN Jesus Christ and believing ON Jesus Christ? The minister thought about it, and finally answered: "To believe IN Jesus Christ means to commit ourselves unto Him in order to be saved, and to believe ON Jesus Christ is to rest on Him with perfect confidence as the foundation of that salvation.

When I first read this story, I was struck by how much truth about God and salvation rests on a proper understanding of the preposition when used with the word "believe". Now, to the second concept that is important to a complete understanding of faith.

Faith vs. Faithful

As you pieced together the many insights into the meaning of faith, you have, no doubt, come to see that the words '*Faith and Faithful*' have a kind of a *ying* and *yang* relationship, i.e., their meanings are somewhat two sides of the same concept imbedded in the Greek usage of the word pistos.

The terms faith and faithful, are so interwoven that to eliminate one is to lose the other. A person's faithfulness to God (or another person) is totally dependent upon ones faith in their words and ability to lead.

As a result, immorality of a Christian leader is grounds for disqualification from ministry. Also, a condition for being selected for spiritual leadership is a track record confirming that the individual is a person who has confirmed the legitimacy of his trust in the Lord with a pattern of faithful behavior.

Faithfulness is in fact an act that responds to an exercise of faith. If we are going to obey the Lord, are we not doing these things because we believe and trust the Lord?

To appreciate how these two terms are "joined at the hip", realize that the word "faithful" may also be translated "a believer", a faithful one, trustworthy, or one on whom we may rely." Also, their linkage is the basis of rewards. To appreciate this, consider one area in which this would apply, stewardship. Giving is an act based on a heart that trusts; therefore, it is not possible to reap the benefits of financial blessings if one is not found faithful with this world's goods?

Then, as a further result, the Holy Spirit, gives that person eternal life. Because it is a pure gift, the apostle described it as salvation by virtue of the grace of God. As a result, Paul describes the true believer as the "faithful" vs. "graceful". It was his way of pointing out a vital fact: the very act of trusting Him results in our sharing His nature, as our new nature, making us people of the Faith.

In the introduction to his Letter to the Ephesians, the Apostle Paul addresses them as, " the saints who are at Ephesus and faithful in Christ Jesus". At the risk of sounding too grammatically technical, permit me to point out a fine point of grammar in order to bless you with a rich spiritual insight.

In this phrase, Paul used only one definite article in order to link the words "saints" and "faithful" into a unified idea. It was his way of describing a saint as a person whose primary function is to "exercise faith by placing his trust in Christ as his only hope and confidence for eternal life, and that *pistos* not only means trusting in Jesus, but it is also doing so in a trustworthy manner by living a trustworthy life. A saint is a person who has not only put his faith in Christ, but he is now one who is trustworthy, consistent, constant, reliable, and faithful. To Paul, God not only demands *faith*; but He also demands *fidelity*.

Unfortunately, today, we see, within the Body of Christ, such widespread unfaithfulness, as disobedience to the Word of God, to service in the house of God, or one's stewardship.

My response to such observations is this: I take stock that my actions match what I preach.

It's All about the Object

One hears people of the post modern persuasion say, such things as "my faith," or "my faith helped me," or "I have faith in faith," or "I was so troubled that I lost my faith." It is because they embrace the false concept that faith is its own object.

Paul would argue that one could no more exercise faith, without having an object for the act of trusting, than one could speak of "driving" and not connect it to a specific vehicle.

By connecting faith to the object of Christ Jesus, the nonsense of "faith-in-faith" for the sake of having a feel good type of religious experience is exposed. Incidentally, modern man does actually place his faith in true objects—money fame, etc.—but not in Jesus as his Savior.

Charles Spurgeon illustrated the importance of faith's object by telling of two men in a boat. Caught in severe currents, they were being swept toward a waterfall. On shore, some men tried to save them by throwing them a rope. One man in the boat caught hold of it and was pulled to safety on the shore. The other, in the panic of the moment, grabbed hold of what looked to be a more substantial object, a floating log that resulted in his death. What the man's faith was connected to made the difference between living and drowning.

Having showcased much data concerning the meaning of *faith,* let's investigate some implications of our many faceted definition of faith.

Elements of Faith

As one might analyze a chemical compound to determine the elements that comprise it, so we can look at the three elements that make up true faith as embodied in the word *pistos*.

The Intellectual Element

Bible scholar, J.Gresham Machen, wrote, "Faith is not merely founded upon knowledge; but it also leads to knowledge". What he meant is that faith has an intellectual component that involves this process: the Spirit, using the Scriptures, speaks to the spirit within man, sharing insights that the intellect then can grasp, which he then does.

But, such an idea requires me to put forth a word of caution: pure intellectual assent is not true faith, and Machen would agree with this assertion. This is the kind of faith that Nicodemus held before he came to Jesus (John 3:2), or that the demons embrace in their limited knowledge of God (James 2:19).

Compare these with the reaction of John after peering into the empty tomb of Jesus (with Peter beside him) "…saw and believed". What his eyes beheld, his mind drew conclusions about, with the result that he exercised true faith in the Lord Jesus, in spite of the fact that he (and Peter) as of that moment did not know, "the Scripture, i.e., that he must rise again from the dead (20:9). John's point is that his faith was, in a flash of insight, built from comprehending certain facts on which he based his faith.

This intellectual element includes belief in the revelation of God in the natural realm; in the historical facts of Scripture; in the doctrines taught therein as to man's sinfulness; the redemption provided in Christ; and the conditions for salvation and blessings as promised to God's children. While this element of faith is greatly disparaged in our day, it is nevertheless fundamental to the other components of faith.

How different from postmodernism, which, like Lord Alfred Tennyson, says that, "We have but faith: we cannot know (its content or object)".

Isn't this just the opposite of what Paul's understanding of faith? This is seen in three passages in his Letter to the Romans:
1. Belief comes by hearing, and hearing by the Word of God. (Rom. 10:17).
2. We know that there is a God, therefore we believe in His existence (1:19, 20);
3. To believe the Gospel one must intellectually understand its meaning (10:14).

Therefore, Scriptural faith is not just an acceptance of a working hypothesis in religion, either in the volitional sense or in the instrumental sense, but it is belief based on the best of evidence.

The Emotional Element

The emotional component is very important because it takes the truth with which the mind has intellectually grasped, and energizes it into a feeling sufficient to move the will to action. Without emotion, the will cannot be sufficiently energized to provoke the person to act.

This process has been beautifully captured in the words of Psalm 106:12, 13; "Then believed they, His works; and they sang his praise. Then they soon forgot his works; (later) they waited for his counsel". Thus, it describes belief that has captured only the heart.

Its New Testament counterpart, Matt. 13:20, 21, describes this same failure as taking place when the seed, being sown upon the rocky places, picturing a person who hears the Word, and joyfully receives it, but fails to allow it to take root within his heart, by briefly embracing it until a problem arises, then abandons his commitment to the truth of the Word. Jesus shared this parable (John 8:30) to distinguish between those who believed on Him (eis auton), and those who merely believed Him (auto).

It is the type of faith that we find so frequently in revivals that lay undue stress on the emotions without seeking a true commitment. Quite often those assigned to follow-up discover that with many (not all) there was an immediate acceptance of Christ and a manifestation of the fruit of the new life; but as in the parable of the sower says, "when tribulation or persecution arose, because of the word, straightway (they) stumbleth". (Matt.13:20, 21 KJV).

While the emotional element is certainly to be recognized as a primary constituent of faith, it must not be treated as if it were the sole characteristic of faith. A reliance on emotion as the evidence of faith tends to produce a condition known as becoming "backslidden". Unstable believers feel they must return, repeatedly, to the "Mourner's Bench", to recapture that same emotional experience to feel "saved".

The Volitional Element

This element of faith is the logical outgrowth of the intellectual and the emotional. If someone accepts the revelation of God and His eternal salvation as true by using both his mind and his heart, then, the next logical step is to act on the truth believed.

Incidentally, not only is each milestone logically important, but, the order cannot be violated: first mind, then heart, then the will.

Unfortunately, a person is not saved unless his faith can demonstrate all of these three elements. However, the volitional element is so comprehensive that it presupposes the other two. This is true because, at this stage, the truthfulness becomes appropriated, through one's spirit, into the center of one's life. This is the best safeguard against "mental ascent", the killer substitute for true faith that can never result in a personal, vibrant relationship with the Lord.

So, faith is the result of certain actions that encompass all aspects of a person's immaterial nature:
1. This person adopts a new mental perspective: He sees the Scriptures as relevant to his needs. He discovers that it suddenly expresses promises relevant to his needs; indicating the conditions for appropriating the blessings of salvation. This is the intellectual aspect of Biblical faith.
2. As a result, he adopts a new emotional perspective: He then sees the promises in the Word as meant for him, personally and specifically. The result is that he starts personalizing his relationship with Jesus by considering the promises as a personal note meant to personally bless him.
3. His prayer becomes a means to faith-building (Mark 9:24; Luke 17:5; 22:32). Nothing can deliver one from a spirit of unbelief and

Faith That Moves Mountains and Smashes Strongholds

strengthen (i.e. increase) one's faith like prayer. Its power to increase one's faith becomes evident when we measure the increase in our ability to trust Him that results from answers to our prayers.

Why then would anyone distinguish some people as possessing a superior quality of faith as compared to the rest of us?

This question was put to the man of great faith. George Mueller of Bristol, England supported 2200 orphans by intercession. His response to the question: "Mine is the same kind of self-same faith which is found in every believer. The growth of this faith has been increasing for the last sixty-nine years from one answer to the next".

It is fascinating to understand how faith operates: beginning with truth understood, valued and desired, and then appropriated by being acted upon, still. It is also important to understand where all this originates from within us. This kind of faith is possible because the believer has a brand new human spirit in which he and the living God can fellowship. This is where faith begins to function.

These three elements are not just involved in everyday decisions of faith they are the keys to making the initial decision to become a Christian. Acquiring true faith involves a process much like falling in love.

Imagine, a young man meeting a young woman for the first time. Immediately, they are attracted to one another. They both say to themselves "Now there is someone I'd like to marry."

At that point, if the emotions had their way, there would be a wedding. But the intellect intervenes, questioning the impulsive emotional response. "Would we be compatible? What is she really like? Can I afford to support her?"

Both individuals conclude that it would be better to take some more time and answer a few questions before they proceed toward the marriage altar. As a result, they begin spending more time with each other. He eventually concludes that she is as beautiful on the inside as she is on the outside. Now his intellect has sided with the emotions on the idea of marriage.

But the final and heaviest vote remains to be cast -- that of the will. It stops any march toward the altar with these questions: "Am I willing to give up this lifestyle for another? What about my freedom -- is it worth the trade? Am I willing to assume the added responsibility?" The marriage will not occur until their wills finally agree with the emotions and the intellect. And so it is in coming to Christ.

Likewise, the decisions that involve true faith involve the mind, emotion, and the will—but the will holds the final key to trusting or not trusting.

It Operates in the Realm of the Spirit

The Christian life begins with the re-creation of the human spirit as a place wherein God, who is a Spirit, can fellowship with man. To help you to understand this, permit me to share some basic theological truths from the Scriptures.

God Is Spirit

To appreciate the nature of true faith and how it should be applied to one's life, listen to the principles that are expressed in this statement by the Lord:

> "But the hour cometh, and now is, when the true worshippers shall worship the Father in spirit and in truth: for the father seeketh such to worship him. God is a Spirit and they that worship him must worship him in spirit and in truth." (John 4:23-24 KJV).

Notice that God is clearly revealed as "a Spirit" – He primarily exists in the spiritual world. The Bible calls Him "The Father of Spirits" (Hebrews 12:9).

Some Christians wrongly place God in one spiritual world and Satan in a totally different one. This may not be openly stated, but it is suggested through some popular religious teachings.

Man's Spirit

The Bible also reveals that we are made up of three primary parts: spirit, soul and body. The Bible calls the human "spirit" the innermost part of us. It also says that it is through this spirit that we personally contact the spiritual world. Before salvation, our human spirit was dead—i.e., completely inoperative. Our new birth resulted in the creation within us of a new spirit. This was to enable us to be able to fellowship with God through the Person of the Holy Spirit. This is what Jesus explained to the Samaritan woman in those verses quoted above (John 4).

Unfortunately, this new spirit becomes a battleground because evil spirits can access it, also. For the true believer, demonic access is only possible through the soul, and that is accessed only through the flesh, and faith will prevent us from acting in the flesh. Another source of protection is the Holy Spirit who takes up residence without our human spirit to guide us into knowing how to apply the truth of the Word to ward off satanic attacks. The use of the Word in this protective manner is described by Paul in Ephesians 6:16 as the shield of faith, which is often called "word of faith". It is a word whose true meaning you understand, and yet, to apply it, you require the anointing power of the Holy Spirit to transform it into something personal, and appropriate for you to apply as an act of obedience and worship.

It was this process that made the Gospel message reach to the center of your being so that you were moved to repent, believe, and receive, by grace, God's full salvation. Also, this word of faith transforms a Biblical promise into a hope engendering force for dealing with problems. All Word, that truly impacts your life is such a word—a Word of faith.

It is such a blessed experience when a Bible study is transformed from being impersonal and intellectual to an experience filled with passionate praise and worship. Is this what Paul was suggesting when he wrote:

> "As ye have therefore received Christ Jesus the Lord, so walk ye in him: Rooted and built up in him, and established in the faith as ye have been taught, abounding therein with thanksgiving." (Col. 2:6-7 KJV).

So, if this concept of the word of faith is so important, on what is it based, and how broad is its scope?

Word of Faith's Base

Biblical faith is founded on God's covenant promises. These promises are rock solid and unchangeable. Religion can undermine Biblical faith by attempting to redefine God's blessings and promises in an effort to cast doubt on God's willingness to do what he says or attempting to rationalize the promises as not fully relevant to your need.

Word of Faith's Scope: Promise for Healing

The Promises of God speak of God's ability and willingness to minister to man's needs; and this includes every aspect of your life—including the healing of the sick.

Jesus spent nearly half his earthly ministry healing the sick not just throughout His earthly ministry, but even after His resurrection. One could correctly add that this ministry continued into His ascension, as He healed through the true believers as the Book of Acts describes:

> "And by the hands of the apostles were many signs and wonders wrought among the people: (and they were all with one accord in Solomon's porch. And believers…brought forth the sick into the streets, and laid them on beds and   couches, that at the least the shadow of Peter passing by might overshadow some of them…*and they were healed every one."* (Acts 5:12-16 KJV).

We should all get down on our knees and thank God for His great mercy to enable His healing power to serve the needs of mankind through His devoted servants. I could not envision my own ministry without the use of this precious and most practical gift, for which I thank God daily.

Unfortunately, there are many who want to limit this with careful phrases. Permit me this personal testimony to illustrate my point. I sat with a pastor as he prayed for a lady possessed with evil spirits.

After the prayer he turned and said, "Now, we need to believe that God will heal you, *if it be His will."* The phrase disturbed me. Would he have said to her, assuming she had been praying to receive Jesus as her Savior,:"Now, we need to believe that God will save you – if it be His will". Of course, knowing this man's doctrinal background, I knew he would have rejected this as bad theology and rightly so because the Bible teaches that it is God's will for <u>all</u> to be saved and come to the knowledge of the truth (1Timothy 2:3-4). But the same Bible also promises divine healing for all, as well.

Why, then would anyone pray (in regard to healing) "if it be your will (O Lord)? My own experience is that such an interjection infects the spirit with doubt that spoils the power and effectiveness of a word of faith. Such doubt subtly perverts Biblical faith into the counterfeit of "wishing" and "hoping" and strips Biblical faith of its power, as the Apostle James described as a "wavering" faith:

> "But let him ask in faith, nothing wavering. For he that wavers is like a wave of the sea driven with the wind and tossed. For let not that man think that he shall receive any thing of the Lord." (James 1:6-7 KJV)

These words expose one of the central reasons the church is powerless today. We have reduced Biblical faith to "religious wishing." God doesn't honor our philosophy about faith—He honors our true faith! True faith must not "waver"; but trust with confident expectation (the opposite of wishful hoping). Real faith is anchored in God's unchangeable promises that infuse it with audacity—the kind that David demonstrated by challenging Goliath.

Did David approach Goliath wishing and hoping for victory? Hardly; instead, he met this giant with the confidence of God's victory—even before the first stone left his sling. That's real faith, and without real faith, we don't receive anything from the Lord. Now where did David get such an idea? The outcome had been promised to Abraham: Goliath challenged the promise of God to give His people the land being fought over.

The promises of Biblical faith remain the same for us today. Yet, sadly, that many true believers choose to weaken these promises into MAYBE and SOMEDAY". Too many professing Christians practice this type of powerless belief. It really reduces faith into nothing more than mental ascent.

Mental assent says, "I agree that Jesus once lived and died on a cross for the sins of the world." Biblical faith says, "Jesus died on the cross for my sins and I trust Him to provide me with eternal life." The difference is subtle but so important: mental assent agrees with the above Biblical fact, but Biblical faith embraces the truth as meant for its own personal need, and thereupon acts accordingly upon it as meant to produce an action that applies the truth of God's Word to one's self. Suddenly the promise has been personalized and that benefit it offered is appropriated.

Thank God for the word of faith, that discovers a Biblical Promise, then lays it before the Spirit to illuminate our mind to see its relevance for us, and fire our heart with His confidence that He will do as the Word promises for us, now and no maybe.

In contrast, mental ascent could not move a grain of sand, let alone a mountain.

Employing a Word of Faith

We suggested a process for transforming a promise into a powerful word of faith. We will now describe the steps that make this possible: to believe, to confess, and to receive. Let's describe these in brief detail.

Step One: Believe
This initial aspect of turning a Biblical promise into a word of faith requires that we embrace the truth of the promise as relevant to our need, and available now. Since the Bible describes God as not only willing for us to approach Him in this manner, but actually encouraging us to do so, it is not presumptive to approach the promises in this way.

Step Two: Confess
This word was well known to Abraham, as well as to the Apostles.
1. The Hebrew word for Confess: *yadhah* means, "to confess, admit, and acknowledge."
2. The Greek word for Confess: " *homologeo* is a combination of *lego*, "to say," and *homos*, "the same thing," to produce our word, meaning, *"to say the same thing"* (i.e., to agree in statement.").

With this essential meaning in mind, we will now seek to understand this word with more depth.

In Romans chapter 10, Paul says that the appropriate confession of a true believer is of Jesus Christ as Lord and Savior (vs.9). In this brief phrase we see that confession has an objective aspect and a subjective one.

The objective aspect involves confessing Christ as the genuine personal Savior of all lost humanity. It recognizes that He is both God, the One who paid the perfect redemption price that enables the Father to accept those who place their total faith in His finished work on the Cross to become His children, i.e., true believers. But there is also a subjective aspect. This involves assuming that this salvation He offers is for you, and acting upon the truth to personally surrender your life in total commitment to Jesus as Lord of your life.

These two aspects must be simultaneously embraced to activate the word of faith. Yet many in the church attempt to separate these two aspects by suggesting that it is possible that one could embrace Jesus as their personal Savior, and only later, confess Him as Lord? Clearly, the faith that results in full relationship requires that the confession include both aspects.

Someone has reduced the process of making a confession that moves the Throne of Heaven to accept and restore you to full fellowship as involving these stages: Repent, Trust (Receive) Forget, Act. Permit me to provide you a better understanding of these important stages.

1. Repent
The Greek word is constructed from *meta* meaning "change," and *noeo*, "mind," to represent the idea of changing one's attitude toward something."

2. Trust
Confession involves speaking words that you believe to be absolutely true; that asking the Father to act on his promise as personally relevant to your need.

3. "See"
In regard to receiving, we need to understand a very important principle: the importance of "Seeing" to receiving a word of faith. In true Believing, as in real life the expression, *"seeing is believing"*, is very true. The principle behind this is that if you can see yourself receiving it, you will receive it. I

like to put it this way: Believing is seeing yourself receiving what you are asking God for. This is the "look of faith". To help clarify my thinking for you, permit me to share the following illustration.

> Two small boys stood on a hillside and studied the setting sun.
> One said, Can you believe how far the sun has moved?"
> The other, "The sun has not moved—we have moved, because this is what Father told us"
> But the brother shook his head, "Naw, the sun did move (for he had observed it) and the earth had not moved (since he had been standing on it). Then he said, "I know what I see", he said triumphantly.
> To which the other boy replied, "And I believe Father.

What a picture of people today, divided over accepting only what their senses reveal to them, and the others believing the Word of the Father, thereby discovering the principle: "believing is seeing"..

How true this is in the matter of faith.

The prayer of faith requires that you must be "totally confident" and "totally convinced" that God has predetermined that you are to be granted your request, without any lurking hint in the back of your mind that suggests to your flesh, "True, this is a promise, but it may not be meant for me".

Holding in one's mind the idea that "God may not think that it's wise for me to have this" is devastating to effective praying,. It destroys the premise of what Jesus is teaching us in "*Therefore I say unto you, whatsoever things ye desire, when ye pray, believe that ye receive them, and ye shall have them.*" (Mark 11:24 KJV). Placing negative conditions on prayer has the tendency to pervert faith into "hoping and wishing". Faithless doubting contradicts the true value of using a promise to get tangible results. Ask Peter, he experienced the consequences of such doubt.

One evening Jesus walked on the water near where the apostles were rowing their boats. Peter asked the Lord for permission to walk on the water to His side. The Lord invited him to do so. Unfortunately, as soon as Peter entered the water, he took his eyes off the Lord, to focus on the rolling waves, and promptly sank until the Lord rescued him. Later, Jesus explained his problem: O thou of little faith, wherefore didst thou doubt? (Matt 14:25-35 KJV)

Peter's failure reminds us of the misguided teaching on faith that leaves everything, (fatally) up to God. True faith succeeds because it is a mixture of correctly understood promises of the Word, plus the exercise of true faith; no faith – no results.

What is the antidote for such poisonous thinking? We must ask the Spirit to enable us to see that a promise IS meant for us, as Hebrews 4:1,2 suggests: :"Let us therefore fear, lest, a promise being left us of entering into his rest, any of you should seem to come short of it. For unto us was the gospel preached, as well as unto them: but the word preached did not profit them, not being mixed with faith in them that heard it."

So, "seeing" means that before the miracle happens, your mind perceives the answer as an accomplished fact. In this regard, you are imitating the Centurion who came to Jesus for a miracle.

His statement shows that he was able to see the miracle as an accomplished fact because he saw it through "the eye of faith": "Lord if you just say the word, my servant will be healed (Matt. 8:5-10). The centurion received the answer <u>before</u> he saw his servant healed. Jesus called this "great faith." This ability is a gift of God, and most important because it is crucial to receiving that you ask of the Lord.

4. Receive

Of course, if you can "see" it as relevant for your life, you then need to "receive", i.e. appropriate it by faith. Perhaps, it will help if we provide you an understanding of the meaning of this word "to receive". This word was also known to the Patriarchs as well as the Apostles. The Old Testament word , *Laqach*, means " "to grasp in order to receive, to acquire".

The New Testament equivalent, 'lambano", means "to take, to bring under one's control". Jesus discussed the importance of this stage when He said (in a great prayer promise), "And all things whatsoever ye shall ask in prayer, believing, ye shall **receive**." Mat. 21.22.

Conclusion

We began, asking the question, *What is Faith*? In these pages we discovered that it is a combination of a certain conviction that we will get the thing(s) we request based on Biblical evidence (promise).

What's In a Word?

Then we explored the ways in which true faith is processed by the human mind, heart, and spirit (will) until it becomes not just a Biblical promise but also a Word of faith that you can use to move a mountain.

Now that we have, in mind, a clear idea of what true Biblical faith is, it seems appropriate to guide our thinking to some of the outstanding men and women who have so effectively model this kind of faith.

PART TWO:
People Who Modeled True Faith

It is axiomatic that if you want to gain a very good understanding of any concept, nothing brings clarity like a real life example.

We have just probed the meaning of faith to significant levels of breadth and depth. Now, we shall look at a few Biblical characters who modeled true faith beautifully. We not only discover how important faith really is, but also how to possess and exercise the kind of faith that God requires, is pleased with, and to whom He stands ready to respond with a blank cheque. In this Section you will meet Biblical figures with stellar abilities to trust the Lord in the darkest hours.

Chapter 2 Abraham, the Father of our Faith
Of course we begin with the man whom the Bible speaks of as the father of our faith.

Chapter 3 Enoch and Noah: Two Men with Death-defying Faith
Show me two men who lived so close to God that they experienced a quality of faith-walk that defied death, and I will show you stories worth probing for their secrets.

Chapter 4 Caleb, a Gentile with an Ageless Faith
Here is a man who came into the family of Israel as an abandoned child, and ended up being rewarded with one of the finest homesteads in the Promised Land, all because he was a man who "fully followed" the Lord.

Chapter 5 Rahab, the Gentile Grandparent of the Messiah

From a lady of the evening to a lady of faith, this woman's perceptive understanding of true Biblical faith resulting in her becoming, by marriage, part of the lineage of Jesus.

Chapter 6 Shadrach, Meshach, and Abednego: Faithful Men Aflame

Next we will focus on three Jewish men whose faith enabled them to survive a fiery death in such a way that the Person in whom they were trusting actually appeared.

Chapter 7 Job: Faith for When the Mountain Falls on You

For our final study we will probe one of the three greatest men of the Old Testament, a Gentile, who, although a contemporary of Abraham, came to faith by a completely different path.

So, with this overview as an introduction let's learn faith from the people who understood it with such clarity that their model becomes our learning event.

Chapter 2

Abraham, the Father of our Faith

No Biblical character ever modeled true faith as Abraham. His unique ability to trust the Lord every day in every way earned him the title, "the father of our faith."

One event in Abraham's life contributed significantly to this reputation. It was that unforgettable moment when he was asked by God to offer up his twelve year old son, Isaac, as a sacrifice. That has to be one of the ultimate tests of faith!

Let us seek to understand how this Patriarch became such a model of the obedience of faith by tracing his history with the goal of discovering this insight.

Roots of His Faith: His Ur Experience

It began in his hometown, a metropolis called Ur. He was asked by the Lord to move his family away from a comfortable life to a new land without being told anything about it except that God would bless him for obeying this call. The author of Hebrews captures his response: "By faith Abraham, when he was called to go out into a place which he should after receive for an inheritance, **by faith, obeyed**; and he went out, not knowing whither he went." (Hebrews 11:8).

Reading this, I try to imagine how obedience would transform many homes, and churches into environments where peace, fairness, and joy dominate. I then considered my own acts of disobedience, when I chose to do my will instead of the Lord's will as an act of faith. Perhaps this was Abraham's experience at one time, but the calling of God at Ur changed his life.

Abraham's life teaches us several things about true faith:
- It is the gateway into a life of blessing (salvation).
- Salvation is a life of blessing
- This life results from bringing your life into conformity with the will of God;
- That will is expressed through the Word of God
- The initial act of trusting Him begins a life of sustained trusting; and
- Living in trusting obedience describes what it means to live the life of faith.

Practicing these principles of faith so consistently, earned Abraham that title.

The obedience that comes of faith is a very noble variety; surely more esteemed than that of a slave, which, by responding to the whip, practices the kind of obedience one might expect from a well-trained dog.

In contrast, consider the obedience, which is rendered from the heart. Does the Lord not consider it as very priceless? Permit me to contrast these two approaches to faith by introducing you to Joe and Mary.

Consider Joe—he obeys because he has no opportunity of doing otherwise, and if, he could be free, he would immediately become a rebel. Therefore, his obedience is practically meaningless.

In contrast, observe Mary. Her obedience springs from faith, energized by the Holy Spirit within her heart without the need for coercion. Its compulsion comes from the passion generated by her trusting heart. What accounts for this kind of faith? She has, within her, the intuitive understanding that she ought to obey her Redeemer, her Father, and her God. At the same time, the love of Christ constrains her to act as she does. As a result Mary is able to perform, with true affection, the very thing that her heart desires. No wonder then, that during times of trials, this sense of great obligation does not abandon her.

When the heart is acting in faith based obedience, as Abraham did, then life has few trials, which can turn the gracious soul from its passion for obedience. Even death cannot diminish this beautiful fellowship, because faith-obedience is also an important component of heaven—where we shall see the face of our Lord, and serve him day and night in his temple. What then is the secret of such faith?

Essence of His Faith: Childlike Consistency

Notice that, in every act recorded of him in Genesis, Abraham's obedience was the result of his act of faith. Surely that principle holds for every act of true obedience for you and me: our obedience is produced by our faith. This process does not vary:

- The Holy Spirit makes clear and relevant a Biblical principle He wants us to obey;
- Then He strengthens us with His unique love and grace to move us to obedience;
- Then, we find our will directing us toward actions that conform to the Word;
- Then the sweet feeling of joy confirming that our obedience pleases the Lord.

This process begins the instant we accept the Lord Jesus by faith, and it never ceases. It is the process the Lord uses to teach us to obey. Also, as we practice it, we discover this principle: the more of faith in Him you possess, the more of obedience to him you will manifest. The truth of this principle raises three questions:

1. What kind of faith produces obedience?
2. What kind of obedience does this kind of faith produce? And,
3. What kind of life emerges from this obedient lifestyle?

We will now explore each of these in-depth.

What Kind of Faith Produces Obedience?

It Begins with Relationship

Surely the Lord, for giving us the gift of salvation, deserves to control our thoughts and actions. This loyalty of our mind is based on faith, and it is a chief prompter to obedience, and grows out of a relationship with Him. Abraham was known as "the friend of God" and surely this accounts for the headwaters of his ability to trust.

It Grows By Trusting His Word

When we get to know Him, we learn that His mind and heart cannot urge us to do anything that is NOT in our very best interest. We become convinced of the rightness of all that God says or does without viewing it as a type of tyranny. We also, learn in our personal relationship with Him that He is infallible, and any fear that His will could be wrong counsel is removed.

Personalizing His will to our Need, Motivates Us to Obey

Abraham's chief concern was to obey the word of the Lord, which the Holy Spirit had delivered to his own soul. Likewise, we should cry, "Lord, what would you have me to do?" Suddenly, we learn that it is the one thing that will bless us. Realizing that obedience serves our interests as well as His own, we become energized to a new passion for obedience and trust in Him. Suddenly we learn another principle: Delighting Him brings delight to our soul!

Another Motivator: We Sense that by Trusting Him, We are doing Something Important

If someone as powerful and pre-eminent as the Lord asks me to do something, I always sense that it was motivated not only by interests, but His! And His mission has to be the most important one. Suddenly, I realize that I am part of something of major, life changing importance. My life, characterized by trust and obedience is transformed from a mundane existence to one of immense meaning and purpose.

What Kind of Obedience Does Faith Produce?

We will answer this question by pointing out certain characteristics of such a faith.

Obedience that is Prompt

Genuine Faith in God Creates a Prompt Obedience. "By faith Abraham, when…called, obeyed." His response reminds us of David, who, in like manner, said, "I made haste and delayed not to keep thy commandments." Obedience is for the present tense: it must be prompt, or it is nothing; it respects the time of the command as much as any other part of it. The germ of unbelief takes root in the soil of such procrastination.

True Obedience Is Practical Obedience

Notice also that Abraham rendered practical obedience. When the Lord commanded him to permanently leave his father's house, he did not say that he would think it over, consult the opinions of others; he just packed up and moved out.

In contrast, modern "easy-believism" proponents choose not to leave the comfort of their families. In fact these are the same people who will put up with anything before risking their own self-interests. If they do consider going forth, they must first know where they are going, and how much to be picked up in the new country. Not so with Abraham. He "went out, not knowing whither he went."

True Obedience Is Rewarding

Note these words, *"'Abraham was called to go out into a place which he should afterward receive for an inheritance."* Do you think that there might be more people who practiced faith like Abraham's if they could see an instant pay-off in it? But that would violate the essential worth of faith. It requires that we first trust; which requires patient waiting. And therein lies the rub—such delay causes many to lose heart and turn from obedience. But there is a reward in trusting the Lord—so how does one see it?

The person of faith approaches obedience with a long view in regard to its reward, considering it is his responsibility to act in faithful obedience, and leave the pay-off to the Lord's discretion. Otherwise, trusting gets ignored as too impractical.

As you reflect on these marks of obedience, you should also understand that they worked for Abraham (and will work for you, also) because they become part of a lifestyle. Although he dwelt in tents and sojourned in a strange land, operating with the above characteristics; and as a result, he was prepared for that fateful moment he and Isaac began to trudge up Mt. Moriah with firewood and knife in hand.

What Sort of Life Resulted from This Faith and Obedience?

Our final question moves us to consider four benefits from practicing a life of obedience.

It Is a Life of Guaranteed "Success"

If success is measured by quality of life that escapes the hazards of personal weakness and folly, then Abraham achieved it, and so can we. Imagine, never failing to obey and leave the results to the Lord? Doesn't this add up to a "winning score"?

It Is a Life Free of Crushing Cares

Suppose you were on the missionary journey with Mr. Stanley, in the center of Africa looking for David Livingstone. As Stanley, your number one concern would be to find a way out of that jungle and into civilization. But, if you were Livingston your top concern would be to obey the Lord's leading. In reflecting on these contrasting approaches to traveling in the jungle, I think you will agree that Livingston's attitude not only simplified his plans, but it removed from his shoulders the burden of having to have all of the answers? As I reflected on this principle, I saw that when I have nothing to do but obey, my path is suddenly mapped out and my decision making process simplified.

It Is a Life of Highest Honor

Abraham is proof that the most glorifying life one can live is by fulfilling the destiny that the Lord has chosen for us. The reason is simple: our life becomes, in effect, "His life", so His glory splashes over onto our own reputation. To appreciate the truth of this, think about soldiers we honor with medals: they were earned by completely obeying the orders of their superiors. Likewise, history bears witness that the people most honored are those who knew their Father's mind, obeyed it, and demonstrated that they have no other ambition than to follow His will.

It Is a Lifestyle That Can Be Replicated

If a life of faith obedience is worthy of living, it is worth passing on to one's children in the confidence that it will bless them as it has us. Fortunately, the best way children learn is through modeling, especially by parents. So, God-fearing parents, take heart that your example is the surest hope for raising godly children.

Now that Abraham has enabled us to understand how to become people of faith, we are ready to learn from the examples of two more giants of faith—Enoch and Noah.

Chapter 3

Two Men with Death-defying Faith

Isn't it ironic that, the next story after Abel, we encounter the biographies of two men who lived so close to God that they experienced a quality of faith-walk that defied death?

I love the way Hebrew Chapter Eleven, that great Hall of Fame for people of stellar faith walks, sums up the lives of Enoch and Noah: "they walked with God".

From reading between the lines of the account of his life in Genesis, I sense that for Enoch, this journey began with the birth of his son. Such newly discovered responsibility certainly can do this. It culminated with an odyssey that so progressively moved Enoch into a trusting relationship so deep that one day, while the man walked the earth, the Lord simply ushered him into His presence.

Likewise Noah's faith preserved him from a global catastrophe, the Flood. In his case, the instrument was a man made Ark, from which he emerged safely with his family. I love the way the writer of Hebrews describes this, "By faith Noah, being warned of God of things not seen as yet, moved with fear, prepared an ark to the saving of his house; by which he condemned the world, and became heir of the righteousness which is by faith."—Hebrews 11:7.

These two spent their lives in such constant communion with the Most High that they could be fully described as walking with God. And yet, in an important way, the two men were studies in contrast. Perhaps this is why we shall investigate each separately even though they shared two distinctions: they pleased God, and both found favor in the eyes of the Lord. But the story lies in the different ways they walked by faith.

Part One: Enoch, the Man Who Walked by Faith Right into Heaven

How indebted we are to the writer of Hebrews for chapter eleven—the great litany of lives of God's people who lived by faith to the point of losing their lives!

In the midst of this chapter, we find these words regarding Enoch: *"By faith Enoch was taken from this life, so that he did not experience death; he could not be found, because God had taken him away for before he was taken, he was commended as one who pleased God"* (Hebrews 11:5, NIV).

To appreciate the background of this statement, let us turn back to the original story, in Genesis 5:22-24 where we read: *"And after he became the father of Methuselah, Enoch walked with God 300 years and had other sons and daughters. Altogether, Enoch lived 365 years. Enoch walked with God; then he was no more, because God took him away"* (Genesis 5:22, 24).

I am sure that you are not surprised when I say that your walk, like mine has, will change as you continue to trust in Christ. 2 Cor. 5:17 supports this idea, *"Therefore, if anyone is in Christ, he is a new creation; the old has gone, the new has come!"* (NIV).

This should cause us to ponder this question: "Is God pleased with me? With the places I choose for recreation? With the books I read? With what I watch on T.V.? With the words I choose, and the topics of my conversations? Is God pleased with the plans I've made for my future?" Have these choices become very different after you came to saving faith in Jesus?

Enoch was taken away from the evil to come: he saw not the flood, nor heard the wailing of those who were swept away by the flooding waters. His was a delightful deliverance from the harvest of wrath, which followed the universal godlessness of the race. It was not his to fight the battle of righteousness to the bitter end, but, by a secret rapture, to avoid death, and escape those evil days in which his great grandson's lot was cast.

Enoch's life exemplified true faith. Unfortunately, we do not know much about the details of his existence. However, we do have a life that exemplified the same quality of faith so that by studying Noah's life, we can also gain insights into the characteristics of Enoch's faith. Think of these men as modeling, like two identical twins, the same stellar faith walk. So as we move on to analyze Noah's faith, we need to be thinking of how its characteristics mirrored those of Enoch's faith.

Part Two: Noah: a Faith Surviving Last Days Nothingness and Catastrophe

Isn't it fascinating that these two people of the first days of earth could teach us so much about how to survive the last days on earth for the true believer?

While Enoch typifies those of God's people spared the final clash of swords at Armageddon, Noah typifies those who will be fully engaged in spiritual combat, bearing themselves bravely amid backsliding and apostasy, until they shall see the powers of evil trodden under their feet as straw is trodden for the dunghill. As the Flood devoured those wicked people of Noah's day, so the Fire will remove the wicked of the last Days.

Noah's life typifies the life of the faithful believer in Christ who bears witness, during evil days, to the true Gospel, and remains steadfast in both his personal walk and the spiritual welfare of his family, enduring unto the end, and when the catastrophe fell upon humanity, he and his family were spared from the wrath, and lived to build a new life on a new earth.

Noah's life offers a glimpse into a faith walk of one who is the Lord's witness during evil days, and lives through them faithfully, enduring unto the end. It was his lot to be delivered from death. The Ark was, so to speak, his coffin: he entered it as a man dead to the old world. Within its storm proof enclosure he floated into a new life, becoming the founder and father of a new race. Today, the Christian baptism aptly illustrates Noah's experience. A Bible verse that is often used at such events all sums up Noah's experience, "Buried in death, and raised into newness of life (Romans). Noah, in the safety of the Ark, and God's promise, passed into a new life.

Two Men with Death-Defying Faith

The value of this up-close look at Noah's faith is that one can gain not only valuable insights into Enoch's faith. The reason for this is simple: both were the result of men being personally discipled by the leading of Jehovah: whose spirit led guidance we would today attribute to the indwelling work of the Holy Spirit

My goal will be to probe into certain aspects of Noah's life to draw general principles about how anyone can enjoy a genuine walk with God, i.e., one who is visited repeatedly and blessedly with gracious favor by God Himself. To this end we will investigate the matter in the following manner:
1. How Faith Gets to Be So Important in a Person's Life
2. The Role that Faith Plays in a Faith-walk, and,
3. How Obedience Creates the Energy to enable you to maintain a life of Faith.

Our goal will be to provide you insights to enable you to experience a quality of faith capable of not just defying death, whether by Rapture, or by casket, but transforming this ugliest reality on earth—physical death—into a marvelous "home-going" experience that more closely resembles walking into a room than being lowered into the ground.

To appreciate Noah's faith, we should first understand how it became so dominant in his life. We begin here because prior to whatever he accomplished, it began with a relationship with God that was a model of trusting obedience. Our question, however, will not just be to find out how this happened to Noah, but to learn how it can be true of our own experience.

1. Faith was Foremost in Noah's Life

A statement in the New Testament says, where one's treasure lies, there his heart can be found. The thing that Noah prized more than anything in his life—that drove him—was his relationship with the Lord. Out of his fellowship with Jehovah, his faith took root and grew to the point it became the passion for all that he did. (That could be said of Enoch also).

For Noah, his faith in the Lord shaped every decision, and motivated all that he did. One could say, that it occupied the place of being the first principle of his life. As a result, the story that describes him so well, properly began with these words, *"By faith,* Noah...."

As I meditate on this fact that everything in Noah's life grew out of his desire to trust the Lord, I feel challenged to ask myself, is this true of my life? Is my daily reaction of one who is resting in the promise of a faithful God?"

Perhaps, you care to jump into this line of questioning and ask if this is true of your own life as well. It's not just a worthy goal to aspire toward, but, in fact, it is a grievous sin to ignore building our life around a faith rest and faith walk before the Lord.

Without faith we are outside of the kingdom of grace, strangers to the commonwealth of spiritual Israel. Think about it, we have neither part nor lot in pleasing God if we do not live by faith.

Yet, praise God, even if the pressures of life have shredded our faith into small morsels the size of a mustard seed (grain of sand), and even though we become able to exercise this small amount of faith in trembling weakness, nevertheless, God considers it sufficient to trigger His mighty hand to act in our behalf.

Think of faith as like an acorn, from which the oak of holiness will grow. Like that handful of corn, true faith can blossom into manifested fruitfulness. Such promise moves us to ask the practical question, "How, then, does this faith become manifest in one's life?

Noah Believed God in his Everyday Life

Faith that dominates a life is one that is very evident in the ordinary experiences of life. The principle Noah models is this: he could never have entered the Ark (and his own deliverance) if he had not, years earlier, began to trust God in every area of his daily existence. I know this to be the case because the Bible says "…he walked with God", and in his common conduct he is described as being "a just man, and perfect in his generation."

Trust me, the only way you can hope to be considered as just in the sight of God is by handling every single daily event as an opportunity to trust the Lord and follow His guidance. This is because, "the just shall live by faith." It is a great thing to have faith in the presence of a terrible trial; but it must begin here: exercising faith with those every day problems and needs. The kind of faith that is sufficient for such needs as: your daily

Two Men with Death-Defying Faith

bread, the care of your family and home; your employment; the faith that triggers answers to prayer; and enables you to transfer every burden from your shoulders to the Lord's.

I invite you to pause for a moment and meditate on these areas. Afterward, please understand that the faith that enables you to say yes to these areas of life listed above, will not come to you all of a sudden, in the dark night, if you have shut it out through all the bright days.

A great preacher wrote, "There is a cult that professes to develop "Latter Day Saints". At the risk of sounding simplistic, permit me to say that I much prefer to be an "Everyday Saint". He meant by this observation, that Faith must be a constant tenant, not an occasional guest in one's life—not just a vocal Sunday faith; but also a vibrant "Monday faith"? That's the kind that, throughout the entire week, you will be enabled to look unto the Hills, to quote the Psalmist, and find the available Hand of the Lord ready to come to your help, or rescue.

Even when alone in your home, alone, and perhaps drifting off to a nap, you need faith, for who knows what that next telephone ring tone will signal. And who knows what temptation might arise in your mind as you sit alone in silence.

I feel that this is the very kind of faith that will make us into men and women of God as it did Enoch and Noah.

By faith Noah took care of every detail of the project before he entered the Ark. This was true because his faith was an everyday experience, dominating his every decision on a 24/7 basis as he built that monstrous boat. Surely, the immensity of that project, along with the sober consequences attached to it, could have created, in him such a sense of purpose that he might have felt he was entitled ignore the "small stuff", i.e. trusting God for his next drink of water, his next nail to secure a piece of timber. But, by "sweating the small stuff", Noah learned to manage "the big stuff".

How we need to open every area of our life to the will of the Lord, our drive-time, our shopping; every mundane detail! True faith operates in the shopping mall as well as in the prayer closet. So, if we care to move up to be a person with a Noah-like faith, we must learn to bring the Lord into every detail of our life.

Noah Believed the Truth of God's Warning

I met a man who had served in the Vietnamese war in which the US was engaged. He told me that he learned on the first day of arriving in the war the key to surviving. A bomb exploded nearby and every person in the tent fell face down on the ground. He, lacking this awareness, failed to respond soon enough. As a friend picked himself up off the ground he said, "Richard, if you want to go home on a plane instead of a "Body Bag" (as a corpse) you better learn to heed the subtle warnings of impending danger. "Soon", this man told me, "I was a quick off my feet onto the ground as any of them, because I learned to pay attention to the signs of danger."

Noah's faith was robust and for two reasons. First, because he took seriously the words of warning from his God, and, second, he considered that it contained a serious threat.

Noah had, in this case, received a promise of salvation (for his family and himself included); but, his respect for it stemmed from paying attention to God's terrible threat that He would destroy all living things with a flood. His faith believed both the warning and the promise. If he had not believed the threat, he would not have prepared an Ark, and so would not have received the promise. Men do not prepare an ark to escape from a flood unless they believe that there will be a flood.

We all love to trust God to fulfill His promises to us; but, what about the warnings? In my ministry I have observed that a person who does not believe that God will cast unbelievers into hell, will not be sure that he will take believers into heaven? I have concluded that if one doubts God's Word about one thing his is not faith in God, but faith in his own judgment, i.e., faith in his own taste.

Noah Believed the Impossible

Furthermore, Noah believed what seemed highly improbable, if not absolutely impossible. There was not a sea where Noah laid the keel of his Ark; there may not have even been a river to float it in.

Then why would this man pursue such a daunting task? Because he was convinced that the Lord had commanded him; and, knowing God as he did, he knew that such a Perfect Mind could never involve him in a fiasco.

Without a faith in the impossible, I fear that the Christian whose faith is in the probable has nothing more than the faith of a Publican. In contrast, a faith resting on the promise that "…with God all things are possible" is capable of building a boat in a meadow, if God directs.

How can I trust Him when I am unable to comprehend how my circumstances will play out? I can meet this challenge if I keep one thing in mind: What the Lord has spoken He is able to make good; and none of his words shall fall to the ground.

How can I trust Him when I am unable to comprehend how my circumstances will play out? I can meet this challenge if I keep one thing in mind: What the Lord has spoken He is able to make good; and none of his words shall fall to the ground.

Noah's Ministry was directed Toward God

Talk about "guts"; note that Noah was alone in his faith. He preached to people who never followed him. His congregation of true believers consisted of his wife, sons, daughters, and their spouses and children—eight in all.

Of course it is marvelous to be able to worship God in the midst of a large congregation vibrant in their faith and boldly singing their hearts out in praise to Him.

But, suppose you are called to plant a new church? I can testify that in those first days, I felt so alone. As I discussed the new opportunity for fellowship with the people who lived or worked nearby, I could see behind their kind words, they held a look in their eye that told me, "What on earth are you doing that for?"

Today, I share the privilege of being part of a significant fellowship. So, I confess, my experience has been nothing compared to Noah's. He ministered in the midst of a multitude that considered him a fool for believing the Lord. That, my friend, is a very toxic environment—it can shred your faith and kill your energy. I report that I have observed many men and women of God who have not survived. Their faith has disintegrated. They have endured failure and ridicule to the point of losing all energy for vocational ministry.

Yet Noah, standing as erect as a chimney that had survived a house fire, labored on, undaunted about being a solitary witness for one hundred and twenty years without one soul willing to enter the Ark with him and his family. What a trial! What a testimony!

How I love to see people seeking to become members of our congregation. The thought of having to preach for one year without a harvest of souls makes me ponder what I should do. Then I contemplate a lifetime of sermons with no converts, the thought makes me. Then I think of this happening to Noah, and my appreciation for this giant of faith really soars!

But if I had to preach for a year with no converts, what should I do? I hope I should persevere, in the name of the Lord God; but what a trial! What if this trial lasted for my entire lifetime—without anyone receiving the Lord as his Savior. I shudder to even think of such a life; yet there is Noah, vibrant on the pulpit on every occasion. I tell you, here was a man of faith! Finally, he obediently entered into the Ark with only his family to help him with the animals and fix roof leaks. What explains his dogged resolve? His confidence was directed at God—not to those about him—and that made his life one of constant abiding in faith.

Am I sharing this with someone who has prayed for years for a rebellious child, or an unsaved spouse, or a backslidden neighbor? I agree that you have persisted for a great amount of time. But think of Noah's 120 years of faithful intercession and be freshly encouraged.

Noah's Faith Paid No Attention to the World about Him

I envision Noah and his family entering the Ark reeking of pungent pine pitch and limited light from a single door as his neighbors jeered,: "Hey, old man, good riddance Finally, we shall be rid of your preaching". Suddenly the door clanked shut and he was gone. Surely, they must have felt they were staring at the largest coffin in history.

Then, before the cheering died down, it began to rain. It was finished, in part, because the world about him had been unable to dissuade him from being faithful to the Lord.

Such a powerful man of faith! What provided much of the energy for his extraordinary ability to trust the Lord? Let me suggest that it was fear that motivated him to such faith.

2. Fear Was the Force behind Noah's Faith

Noah's faith was based, in part, on the fact that he feared to disobey God in any way. This fear is actually a factor to energize his faith, as the Bible declares, "By faith Noah, being warned of God of things not seen as yet, *moved with fear.*" What kind of fear was this?

Noah's Fear Was Not Based on Intimidation or Reprisal

This is not the fear induced by a bully. Rather, this is that kind of fear that a devoted son carries for his father; whose trust, affection and devotion compel him to fear ever to displease the man he loves, causing him pain or grief.

Unlike a person who fears God as a culprit would fear a judge, Noah's confidence of his favor with the Lord motivated him to be ever careful to offend the One who loved him, and who feared to trifle with matters as important as eternal salvation. Such fear moved him to construct that boat; for he saw it as the very instrument that would save his family; and in the process he found comfort that he was fulfilling God's will for his life. Which raises this question: if his fear was not based on intimidation, then, on what was it based?

Holy Fear Is Based on Loyal Reverence

Perhaps it will help you to appreciate what we are saying if you substitute the phrase "loyal reverence" for the word *"fear"*.

How does this type of loyal reverence translate into a motivation to serve the Lord in trust? He was motivated by a fear of Divine judgment on sin. Perhaps, seeing a jeering passerby as a person who would someday sink to his death beneath a large wave, he was moved to an emotion that was a mixture of holy awe of God, and a dread of the judgments which sin was drawing down upon the giddy world about him.

Noah had a humble Distrust of Himself

I wish we all had such a fear that moved us to fear God because of his greatness, sprinkled, also with a fearful distrust of our own tendency toward sinfulness that provokes us to fear ever falling into sin, and perishing with the rest of lost sinners. Tragically, after the Flood, he did succumb to a terrible sin. But, prior to the Deluge, his healthy distrust preserved his ministry.

I draw great encouragement from Noah's experience. His story makes me realize that no one should ever boast, "Not me, I shall never fail the Lord and fall into sin". It motivates me to stand in daily fear lest I be guilty before God. Is this true of you, dear reader? Perhaps you are a person who operates with a healthy fear of the wrath to come. Realize then, that since you have faith enough to fear, then, that fear can become the catalyst to increase your faith. A holy fear will put wings upon your heels, and help you to reap the fruit of such serious minded fear.

3. The Fruit of Noah's Faith

Faith grafted upon faith produced much fruitful ministry for Noah. How did fear cause faith to blossom into such a powerful faith? Such results occur when certain conditions are met.

His Ministry Changed the World

Think about preaching for one hundred and twenty years without ever seeing one person come to repentance! Add to that this burden: spending one hundred and twenty years building a huge ship as a solution to an impending global Flood in a land that had never experienced rain. But his ministry truly changed the face of civilization.

He was saved and his house

Oh, that God would give to every preacher of righteousness this full reward—himself and his house! Nothing is more important nor a source of greater joy than to know that our children walk in the truth!

Yet I fear that these words strike some heart who would confess that their home is the source of their worst enemies. My advice, "Hold on; trust the Lord; remain faithful, and refuse to doubt the Lord for the answers to your prayers" Make it the most important business of your life. Draw strength from the situation of the Philippian jailer, to whom Paul said, "Believe on the Lord Jesus Christ, and you shall be saved, *and your house.*" Do not rest content with half the promise, but, rather, grasp firmly the words, "and your house."

He was vindicated by the entire world

Notice the text: "By which he condemned the world. During a lifetime of preaching the Gospel he had pronounced condemnation; but, at the end, with the offer of salvation and hope. But, with the waters above their rooftops, no hope remained. Do you think any of those heads bobbing in those fatal waters recalled one of their favorite 'Noah jokes'?

In that final instant, they knew, the man had been correct all along; but now there remained no further opportunity to embrace it and enter the Ark. Actually, it was the Ark that condemned them—the very enormous floating box they stared at from the waves just before they drowned.

When the water reached knee deep, did pound on the door of the Ark? Perhaps they then fled to the mountains trying to flee the relentless water of God's judgment.

One is tempted to view the man's congregation as so tiny that it could not have any impact on anyone. If your church seems so small, take heart from the example of Noah—with a congregation of eight, he changed the world. Like him, may your faithful ministry find honor and vindication!

He became heir of the righteousness, which is by faith

The last thing Noah earned by his faith was this, he became heir of the righteousness. This blessing comes to the person who lives by faith. Listen to these marvelous words spoken to him as he stepped through the door into the Ark by the Lord Himself, "(Noah) "You have I seen righteous before me in this generation." Wow! God declared him righteous; not righteous by human assessment. What a testimony that a life of faith lived out in faithful obedience will earn the most precious words a true believer will ever hear, spoken by the Lord, "Well done, though good and faithful servant."

Noah believed God, found grace in the eyes of the Lord and received the righteousness which God gives through Jesus Christ to all them that believe. Wrapped in this "well done" he stood before the Lord, justified and approved.

The testimony of Noah and Enoch are all the more remarkable because they had no more Gospel truth than that which was spoken in the Garden by the Lord Jehovah regarding the woman's seed, the Lamb's sacrifice. He had no Torah, no Psalms, no Pauline Epistles—but the man embraced all the truth available to his generation from the Lord and acted on its every word. He saw the dark clouds as the approaching judgment of the Son on the serpent; and God honored his faith, condemning the world in the process.

He lived when the rest perished. He was secure in his Ark when the myriads were sinking in the Flood waters: he became "heir of the righteousness which is by faith" when others were condemned.

How indebted we are for the testimonies of Enoch and Noah, two men whose lives were consumed with a passionate faith that led them to walk before the Lord with such perfect diligence that they never feared the worst calamity, including eternal judgment and death.

Chapter 4

Caleb, a Gentile with an Ageless Faith

Introduction

In the well-known story of the reconnaissance of the Promised Land, Moses sent twelve spies to check out the land of Canaan. For forty days they spread out; each scouted a section of this new land and then, rendezvousing, returned home.

The majority report was offered by ten spies who said the place was not worth dying for, since it was infested with grasshoppers and giants. The minority report, offered by Joshua and Caleb, agreed with the ten that the land, indeed, did present gigantic challenges. But, in contrast to their brethren, they saw the situation with the eye of faith, i.e., as an opportunity for God to bless and cause success.

The reports occurred in public and things turned ugly. Yet, here, in this moment of conflict, we first encounter the heart of this man of faith, Caleb. Notice how the Bible describes him: (He) "quieted the people before Moses", and said, 'Let us go up at once, and occupy it; for we are well able to overcome it'" (Numbers 13:30).

Caleb based his reasoning on this fact, "If the Lord delight in us, then he will bring us into this land, and give it us because He has promised it to us as the seed of Abraham" (Numbers 14:8).

So how did the people take his report? They tried to kill him.

To understand Caleb's faith, one needs to understand two statements made about him that tell you much of what made him such a man of faith. They are part of God's testimony –His pronouncement of blessing upon the man:

> "But My servant Caleb, because he has a different spirit and has followed Me fully, I will bring into the land into which he went and his descendants shall possess it.

Caleb was a man of a "different spirit", and he was a man who followed the Lord fully". Let's analyze these two expressions.

A Different Spirit

To understand this phrase we will dissect it into its two component words.

The spirit that possessed Caleb was based on a combination of factors. First, it included the attitude created by having to endure forty years of desert wandering—due to the sin of unbelief by his cohorts. Then, there were the additional forty years spent helping Joshua and the army conquer the land of Canaan. Eighty years, and his spirit remained steadfast.

What accounted for its steadfastness? I think two things energized it. First, he was aware of the promises that God had first made to Abraham (Gen. 17:18), which he, by faith, embraced as a promise rightly belonging to him.

Second, he had implanted in his mind, like a snapshot kept in a shirt pocket, the vision imprinted on his memory by his first glimpse of that part of Canaan he had been appointed to inspect—the hills around Hebron.

Surely the hope that it could someday become the front yard of not just his own home, but the homesteads of his extended family was also a contributing factor that produced the spirit that motivated him for those eight decades.

It is the spirit that blends the promises of the Word, with a vision of a blessed future, with an unwavering, whole-hearted trust in the God of Israel, especially in His Word (promises). That is what made up his spirit.

Now let's examine the adjective, "Different" that describes this spirit. The Hebrew word means, "to close the gap". It is a phrase used by hunters stalking game for an evening meal. Imagine a hunter; he spots an animal and then begins to quietly close the gap between himself and his supper. Get the picture?

Here is a man who, from the time that God pulled him out of the slave pits of Egypt, and transformed the waters of the Red Sea into a gateway into life of abiding fellowship, never allowed anything—huge or small—to get between him and the thing he was stalking. And what was he stalking? The prize was the blessing of God embodied in the Abrahamic promises. To my mind, Caleb lived like the man in the New Testament who continually…" looks to Jesus as the author and finisher of his faith". (Heb. 12:1-4) rather than be distracted by the circumstances about him.

It was a long process, in which, for forty years he had to endure suffering that had befallen him through no fault of his own, but by the judgment of God on the faithlessness of the ten who reconnoitered the land with him. Yet through this arduous process, the man never blamed God but simply trusted Him by waiting for the day when he would be allowed to cross over to the Promised Land.

Now "fast-forward" to that long awaited day when the promise was to become reality. Joshua, perhaps concerned about the man's health asked him if he still wanted to take the hills of Hebron as his own. This senior citizen practically ran up the hill to rout the enemy and move his family into their new home. Because of his great faith, Caleb was blessed (Joshua 14:13-14)!

One might argue, "Hey old man, how are you going to make it up that hill—where will you get the strength?" Caleb's answer might have been, "I lacked the strength 85 years ago to conquer this hill in my own person. As then, so now I will rely on the strength of the Lord. The strength He would have provided for me then, He will supply to me now.

I see this grey haired man leading the attack up Hebron hill with a sword in one hand and a deed in the other and a great-grandson perched on his shoulders! What a man of faith.

In retrospect, Caleb did face all of the enemies the other ten spies' report focused on. Let's look at each some of the problems he encountered as a senior citizen practicing his faith.

Faith That Moves Mountains and Smashes Strongholds

Solomon, in Ecclesiastes 12:5 describes the three characteristics that plague most senior citizens. The first: "The grasshopper becomes a burden". It is a metaphor for the fact that with some elderly people, little things are seen as burdens to bear. It's true, as we get older, the little things can really become a nuisance to us.

A second: (seniors) "are afraid of heights." is a figure of speech for the fact that in old age, men become fearful to take risks—a fear of the challenge of new things.

A third problem that senior believers have to deal with is this: They "glory in the past" at the expense of the present and future

Granted, every age has its difficulties to deal with; and Solomon wisely points out the three that tend to pester those of us in our autumn years: we tend to allow little things to become a real burden; we tend to avoid challenge and risks; and we find it more fun to focus on the past than to plan for the future.

In reflecting on this, I am reminded of something I read recently:

> I get up each morning, dust off my wits,
> Pick up the paper and read the obits.
> If my name is missing, I know I'm not dead.
> So I eat a good breakfast, and go back to bed.

Not so with Caleb! Even in his twilight years, Caleb still possessed a "different spirit", God "fully". Dear senior citizen reading this, are you now convinced from this courageous warrior, that there is no retirement from the Lord's army?

At 85, Caleb had the attitude of a young man. To appreciate it, consider these three realities facing this man in his "senior years"

First, the land he desired to homestead was inhabited by Anakites, a race of giants who arrived in Canaan hundreds of years before the Israelites ever arrived. In fact, throughout the first five books of the Bible, the Anakites are referred to as the enemies that were impossible to conquer.

Second, Hebron was mountainous—the hardest terrain to conquer in battle.

Third, the territory was fortified by cities like Jericho.

Yet, in spite of these challenges, this magnificent old man specifically asked for that portion of real estate. Hey, this was no retirement haven,

"Golden years Manor" the man dreamed of inhabiting. Caleb had no intention of sitting on some veranda, seated in a rocking chair, musing on past glories.

He could have pondered the memory of beholding the ocean floor under the Red Sea which he used for a roadway, or the flurry of dust as the walls of Jericho burst into chards from a deafening trumpet blast that made every ear in a mile to ring. No thank you—Caleb could not drift into yesteryear reveling, for his mind was fully occupied with the contemplation of that next hill he would lead his family to attack at sunrise.

Even in his twilight years, Caleb still possessed a "different spirit"—a spirit of following God "fully". This prevented him from complaining or shirking from the task at hand. So, for forty years, he dreamed of a day when he and God would drive out the heathen of the land. Dear senior child of faith, are you now convinced that there is no retirement from being a soldier in the army of faith?

What drove this man to be such a model of the attitude of the senior citizen as a person of faith? His faith was fired by two things: he was a Gentile; and to him, Hebron was love at first sight. The answer to that important question may surprise you.

Caleb was a Gentile.

When the twelve spies were chosen, all of their pedigrees were listed. Of Caleb's heritage we discover that he was the "son of Jephunneh the Kenizzite, a clan that was not part of the Hebrew nation. Caleb was a foreigner, a Gentile. How did he get mixed up with the Jews in Egypt in the first place?

The text provides a clue. His name means, in English, "dog". It suggests that originally, his parents despised him (reflected in the despicable name they gave him). This being true, it makes sense that they would have abandoned him, or sold him into slavery, no doubt to a Jewish family. It must have seemed a terrible turn of chance. Yet, ultimately, in the providence of God, he participated in the Exodus along with the Israelites, having been, since childhood, part of a Jewish home.

In light of this background, it becomes clear that when he was given, by the Lord, a very 'prime' piece of real estate, he must have treasured it as showing that God had not only invited him into the family as a full participant, but, later, provided not only a new life away from Egypt, but also some of the choicest real estate, next door to those whose lineage carrying the seed of the Lord Jesus. From the very place he settled, Judah, many Kings would emerge. Caleb, a Gentile, became a member of the Jewish aristocracy, since from his land of Judah many kings of Israel came, not to mention key military leaders.

Small wonder, then, that his heart soared with devotion to the living God, since he knew well what it meant to be despised by earthly parents and kicked out into the street, and sold into slavery. As I reflect upon this I am struck with the notion that he represents those to whom God, "…defends… the fatherless and the widow, and loves the alien, giving him food and clothing."

The man truly understood the magnificence of grace, and as a result, this Gentile became a devoted faithful follower of the God of Abraham, the covenant keeping God as his Savior.

And, among the twelve Spies, he was the lone foreigner, yet more passionate about the God of Abraham than his own seed. None of them had his measure of faith in God's power.

Caleb Loved Hebron at First Sight

Focus on Caleb, the outsider being blessed to be included as part of the people of Israel. Then try to imagine how he felt when he first laid eyes on Hebron during his spying expedition. I think he must have felt like a young man encountering the girl of his dreams, whereupon, at first sight, he fell madly in love with her.

For Caleb, from that moment on, the memory of the abundance (milk and honey, and grape clusters so immense it took two men to carry them) and green lush wooded hills with streams running through them he had seen in Hebron was permanently etched on his brain.

Combine that discovery with the connection with his past history. As a child, no doubt homeless and hopeless, and suddenly part of something miraculous and extraordinary, he wanted to get as close to that heritage as possible. Certainly, Hebron had it all. It was, in fact, the very spot where God had first made the promise on which he bet his life to Abraham. It was so favored by Abraham that he buried his wife there, and later joined her in entombment. Later, his sons would be buried there. So, before Caleb ever drew breath, Hebron was a place with a rich spiritual heritage. It just had a slight problem—it was controlled by a barbaric race of giants, the Anakims. Their attachment to it was both pleasurable and because the evil one who controlled their lives from the center of their spirits, Satan, saw it as a way of preventing the blessing promised to Abraham to be realized by his offspring, Israel.

So Caleb vowed, by faith, to become its deliverer and caretaker; smitten by its lush lovely abundance, he sought to possess it as something to be treasured as a pearl of great price.

Therefore, that day did dawn when he went to Joshua and said,

"You know what the LORD said to Moses the man of God at Kadesh Barnea about you and me. I was forty years old when Moses the servant of the LORD sent me from Kadesh Barnea to explore the land. And I brought him back a report according to my convictions, but my brothers who went up with me made the hearts of the people melt with fear. I, however, followed the LORD my God wholeheartedly. So on that day Moses swore to me, 'The land on which your feet have walked will be your inheritance and that of your children forever, because you have followed the LORD my God wholeheartedly.' "Now then, just as the LORD promised, He has kept me alive for forty-five years since the time He said this to Moses, while Israel moved about in the desert. So here I am today, eighty-five years old! I am still as strong today as the day Moses sent me out; I'm just as vigorous to go out to battle now as I was then. Now give me this hill country that the LORD promised me that You yourself heard then that the Anakites were there and their cities were large and fortified, but, the LORD helping me, I will drive them out just as He said." (Josh. 14)

On this important day when it came time to divide the Promised Land, our hero of faith asked for, and was given, the portion of land that had been promised him over eight decades earlier. Even that fact reflects a reward acquired by faith by the Lord extending their lives so that when this day finally dawned both men would have the strength to do what was necessary to claim the land God had promised them decades earlier.

Faith That Moves Mountains and Smashes Strongholds

Dear reader, think about this: according to these characteristics, How "old" are you? You see, ultimately age is not a matter of the physical but the mental; not arteries but attitude. While we all will physically age, we need not age in our spirit, i.e., in our ability to live the life of faith.

As someone once put it, "You are as young as your faith, as old as your doubt; as young as your self-confidence, as old as your fear; as young as your hope, as old as your despair." To win in our battle with aging you and I must know that aging is not just a physical thing. It's an attitudinal thing. It's a choice!

Dr. Paul Brand, a well-known doctor and author, was raised in India. His parents were missionaries there. In his book, *In His Image,* he describe his mom, age 75, still walking many miles each day to visit villages to share the Gospel of Jesus. Then she fell and broke her hip. She lost the feeling in both legs. Her son found her dragging herself by two makeshift crutches. He suggested that she retire from her ministry. She turned around and said, 'What value is it if we try to preserve this body just a few more years and it is not being used for God, what value is that?'" So she bought a donkey and continued her traveling ministry for another 18 years!

Are you getting older? Would you like to slow down the process? Take it from Caleb: living by faith will keep you young and alive. Confidence in the promises of God, and a feeling that he has a purpose for your life is better than the fountain of youth. It will transform your 85th birthday into a college-like commencement. It will transform the chorus you enjoyed as a child into a new song:

Jesus loves me, this I know/ Though my hair be white as snow.
When my sight is growing dim/ Still He'll bid me trust in Him.

When my steps are oh, so slow/ With my hand in His I'll go/
On through life, let come what may, He'll be there to lead the way.

When I am no longer young,/ I'll have much which He's begun/
I will serve Christ with a smile/ Go with others the extra mile.
Yes Jesus loves me! Yes Jesus loves me!
Yes Jesus loves me! The Bible tells me so.

That is the song of a Caleb! He is living proof of the promise in Isaiah in 40:30-31? "Even youths grow tired and weary and young men stumble and fall; but those who hope in the Lord will renew their strength. They will soar on wings like eagles; they will run and not grow weary, they will walk and not be faint."

So what can we learn from this man with the ageless faith?

Caleb never doubted the verity of the promises of Yahweh. He believed with all his heart and soul that Israel would inherit the land which God had promised them. So, what can we learn about faith from this Godly warrior? Let us examine some of these things.

Faith in God Repudiates Ungodly Fear

An optimist sees an opportunity in every calamity. A pessimist finds a calamity in every opportunity.

Caution is prudent if followed by action. But fear doubts the supremacy of the divine arrangement; it questions the wisdom and love of the LORD. Fear paralyzes.

Israel had heard much about the land of milk and honey. They were now at the borders of this Promised Land. Their yearning for Egypt was past. All that remained was the conquest. The spies gazed upon the vineyards and olives groves. They saw the richness of the grain in the fields. They pictured their own farms dotting the valleys. They were excited about each wonder before them. In short, they desired their blessings.

But then they saw the Canaanites, some of them were eight feet tall; they were a symbolic representation of mountains. They looked like the dreaded Nephilim of antediluvian days. In sheer panic, ten spies returned to the camp of Israel with their faith shattered, bearing a message of utter and hopeless despair. Only Caleb and Joshua remembered to "Fear not, neither be discouraged" (Duet. 1:21) because their faith in God remained strong.

Often times in the natural world God's promises to us appear impossible, but we must remember that we walk by faith and not by sight. Thus we are not to concentrate on how it appears in the natural, but, rather, keep our focus on Christ as the author and the finisher of our faith.

Despite what the natural portrayed, Caleb's warrior spirit reflected a kind of warrior faith – persistence, Caleb fought for what he believed – God's promise to Israel.

Afraid, Discouraged, Angry

The congregation of Israel believed the ten men, and even tried to stone Caleb and Joshua to death. (Num. 14:10). What a picture of people abandoning their faith in the Almighty's promise. They cried all night. There is a mentality which says, "Blame it on the leader." The people decided to depose Moses and set up another leader who would take them back to Egypt.

Faith Requires Action

In Numbers 14:6-9, we read that Caleb and Joshua "rent their clothes." They urged the people, "Do not rebel against the LORD. Do not be afraid of the people of the land. We will swallow them up. The LORD is with us."

Nor did Caleb's boundless faith deter him from exerting his physical prowess when waging war against Jehovah's enemies. He is the type of man whom James described, "What doth it profit… though a man say he have faith, and have not works? As the body without the spirit is dead, so faith, without works is dead also" (Jas. 2:14, 26).

Caleb's Strengths

At the age of 85, Caleb was still a strong soldier. He drove out the Anakim from Hebron. (Josh. 14:6-15; 15:14) He then attacked Debir, southwest of Hebron. This conquest was a difficult challenge, so Caleb offered his daughter Achsah in marriage to the valiant warrior who would obtain the victory. Othniel won Achsah and a southland and upper springs and nether springs. (Josh. 15:15-19. This young man later became one of the Judges of Israel, so Caleb continued to serve the people through his heirs.

Caleb lived a life of discipline and self-control. He never permitted himself to become soft. He maintained his assurance in the presence and power of Yahweh; this perspective prevented him from frittering away his physical well being through tension and stress. The sterling faith which characterized his life remains a beacon light, shining for the encouragement of all lovers of God forever.

Caleb's Reward

God said, "No one who has treated me with contempt will see [the Promised Land]. But because my servant Caleb has a different spirit and follows me whole-heartedly, I will bring him into the land he went to, and his descendants will inherit it" (Num. 14: 23, 24).

So what happened to his detractors? They perished in the desert, struck down with a plague. Is this the kind of circumstance that the writer of Hebrews had in mind when he wrote, "The just shall live by faith… (but if any man draw back, my soul shall have no pleasure in him" (Heb. 10:38).

Bottom line: "And Joshua blessed Caleb, and gave him Hebron for his inheritance" (Josh. 14:13). And God will do for you if you, no matter what the calendar says about your body clock, become a person with a faith like Caleb's—an ageless faith.

Chapter 5

Rahab: Messiah's Gentile Grandparent

An unsophisticated man saw a lovely vase in a store window, and bought it. When it was placed on the table in his humble apartment, its loveliness motivated him to straighten up his dingy room. He then washed the filthy drapes, repaired the chair with the stuffing hanging out repainted the walls, even re-gluing the wallpaper. Eventually, the entire room was remodeled—thanks to the transforming influence of a vase.

That vase, impacting that room, is a snapshot of what happened to a Gentile woman, a prostitute, when her heart was transformed by faith in the living God.

Jericho was the second campaign in Joshua's plan to conquer the Land promised to Abraham's heirs. The battle was considered militarily strategic, because with its capture, Canaan would be divided into two separate theatres of war—and people in the northern half of the territory would be unable to help comrades in the southern half.

Such importance necessitated that Joshua have good data on which to make a plan of attack. So he sent out a small band of spies to reconnoiter the city, walls and all.

But the battle was a partnership between people and God; so, in the process of investigating the city, the spies knocked on the door of a prostitute. This tactic made sense because they needed to investigate the walls; and she lived in an apartment built into the walls. Also, she was a known prostitute so no one would question strange men knocking on her door. In fact, the move was not just a good strategy; it was providential.

Brace yourself, the woman who answered that door was the woman whose DNA would appear in two generations in the most extraordinary King to serve the these conquering people—David. Which means the rough looking woman their eyes fell upon would contribute to the gene pool of the Messiah. Isn't it breathtaking just what can appear in the doorway that is willing to open itself to accept the will and grace of God?

Once inside the premises, the spies discovered that God had already been working in her heart. The woman, having heard of their previous success in war, was prepared to become an ally. Her words also showed them that God was going before them to prepare the way for victory. Rather strange turn of events for a house of prostitution wouldn't you agree?

The transformation of this woman can be traced along three major milestones.

- Before Transformation—"Lady of the Evening
- Preparing for Victory—Warrior of Faith, and
- In her new family—Link to the Messiah

What a testimony to the power of God to transform any life that comes to Him with genuine repentance and faith.

Rahab, the "Lady of the Evening"

Face it; the woman participated in a very evil lifestyle. She conducted her business at home in full view of her children. To add to her misery, her family was facing impending disaster as a powerful army camped within striking distance. The end was near!

Before the spies knocked on her door, her life was modestly secure; her family remained fed and secure in the apartment in which men traipsed in and out every day. Then she learned of this people who had defied and crushed the Pharaoh of Egypt.

I find her situation typical of many desperate people, secure in making their living exploiting sin needs of others, and justify it by saying, they are jut supplying a need in a lawful manner.

But standing before these spies, Rahab gained knowledge that she saw as providential and acted upon. It was a great step of faith.

However, Rahab possessed a knowledge she was willing to act upon, by faith. Perhaps it was demeanor of these men (not there for the usual reasons), or the report she had heard repeatedly of Israel's power and its reason as due to a special relationship it enjoyed with the living God. I choose not to speculate further; suffice it to say that the woman chose to act on the truth she knew. (If only churchgoers would follow her suit and act on the truth they know but too often they stubbornly refuse to embrace it let alone act upon it).

So, in the strangest conversation ever held in a harlot's bedroom, these people engaged in a sharing of the Gospel, with a woman responding in true faith, and being transformed into a woman with a pure heart, and an unblemished record of sinless ness before the throne of heaven. How did this woman of filth become a woman of faith?

Rahab, a Sinner Saved by Grace

She Heard the Gospel

She heard the word about the God of Israel. It was a message of judgment that she heard, but it introduced her to the true and living God. The message that fell upon her ears had to have seemed like a ticket to a new life! I've shared this same message of hope and salvation being received by thousands, enough, people to recognize that her reaction was a mark of those who are genuinely regenerated. It is the mark of pure joy.

She Responded to the Message

It is one thing to hear words being communicated to one's ear. It is another thing to really HEAR the message—and this is exactly what she did. I know she really connected with the truth, embracing it in faith, by the way she was moved to address the God of Israel by using His covenant name, YHWH, i.e. "the LORD".

She even described Him as the God of heaven and earth. Another clue that she fully understood the message and her faith was genuine: when the conversation concluded, she described her source of hope in salvation as the word of those who had spoken to her. To Rahab, the words of the spies held the power of the Gospel. No wonder she made the Hall of Fame in Hebrews Eleven—listing the Old Testament giants of faith.

I relish this story because it encourages me with the power of the Gospel to change a life—no matter the situation. Perhaps her lifestyle helped in this process because she could not, by any stretch of the imagination claim she was good enough already, and while not quite ready to accept the Lord Jesus as her Savior, would consider it later, as many upstanding lost church-goers do at every evangelistic service..

Rahab a Warrior of Faith

Suddenly these men were looking at a changed woman. That woman, willing to bare her soul to the utter nakedness of repentance, now stood before these men and her family as a changed woman, a new creation in Christ Jesus. Of course it was a miracle!

How do we know that the Gospel, and not just an attitude seeking hope against certain death by an impending army, whose representatives were there, genuinely changed her life? After all, she was a woman who made a life for herself and her family by trading in favors.

Evidence of her Changed Life

Here are evidences one can consider as proof of her soul's transformation.

She Became a Willing Worker

Suddenly this enemy of the people of God was eager to serve the cause of the Kingdom, and, at great personal sacrifice and personal risk. She was even willing to die for her new faith. As a result, she hid the spies and sent her own leaders off in the wrong direction searching for them. Perhaps this is why James used her as an example of the believer who proves their salvation by the works of their life, James 2:25.

It remains so today: upon receipt of grace that results in salvation, what is the next thing one encounters: "for by grace are you saved…unto good works…" (Eph. 2:8-10). So, Rahab's changed life led her to pursue good works.

She Had a Heart for the Lost 2:12, 13)

Immediately, Rahab became concerned about her family; she wanted the same assurance for them, and, as a result, took steps to reach out to bring them into this new hope.

So, from these simple sentences in Joshua 2 we discover a woman who is genuinely saved. Now let's briefly sketch out the benefits her faith delivered to her and her family.

Benefits of Saving Faith

Now, let us examine some of the benefits that accrued to this woman as a result of her saving faith. Actually, the Bible declares that about forty wonderful things came to her as a result of her decision to become a true believer. But we will mention only four.

Saved from Destruction of Jericho.

Apparently, when the walls tumbled to the ground in pieces, the tiny section in which she had her household, remained intact. It was not hard to find; a scarlet rope hung from its window. It's a picture of how the souls of the redeemed are marked by the blood of the Lamb covering their sin, marking them for salvation instead of eternal destruction. So this woman, experienced some important benefits of her new relationship with God in the here and now (vs. the sweet by and bye).

Discovered a New Family

After the battle was over, she and her family joined the people of Israel and married into one of their Tribes and became integrally involved in their covenant blessings. She was spared the lifestyle and the hopelessness and alienation that had been her lot in that Jericho brothel. What a testimony of God's graciousness in salvation!

Gained a New Type of Reputation

In one act of redemption, Rahab moved from being a woman of shame to a woman of spiritual fame. She actually became the ancestor of Jesus, since she married the great-great grandfather of David. (Matt. 5). Think about it, in His lineage it was a Gentile harlot who was transformed by His grace. Imagine, the remarkable climb from the gutter to the throne.

She Gained a Heritage

Also, because she placed her faith in the Lord God of Israel, she obtained some precious possessions. Notice how God took this former harlot and blessed her new life with the richest of His blessings. She became the woman God's sovereignty chose to provide key DNA to produce David, Solomon, and eventually the Son of God.

What made Rahab different from the other people of Canaan? The evidence that the God of the Israelites was indeed the God of heaven and earth convinced her; and she was moved by faith to submit to that evidence (Matthew 7:21; Romans 6:17; Hebrews 5:9). Jesus said, "If any man will do his will, he shall know of the doctrine, whether it be of God, or whether I speak of myself" (John 7:17).

Let us be people with willing, submissive hearts, ready to submit to God's Word. The writer of Hebrews tells us, "But without faith it is impossible to please him: for he that cometh to God must believe that he is, and that he is a rewarder of them that diligently seek him" (Hebrews 11:6).

Concluding Thoughts

Everything that Rahab had heard reinforced the fact that this God of the Israelites does what He says He will do. It was her hope that if she could somehow come under His people's protection that she would escape the coming destruction of Jericho.

Rahab knew that the only way she could obtain this protection from the destruction of her entire household was to risk everything. In order to have faith in God, she had to lose faith in everything else! Rahab could have exposed the spies and then benefited from the reward for their capture.

However, Rahab had heard about the Israelites and their God, and chose to base her decision on this knowledge. This is an excellent example of trusting in the word of the Lord; and by a woman of pagan Jericho; a prostitute, living on the edge of town within the city walls. Rather, Rahab based her faith on the God who does what He says He will do, who keeps His promises, and who protects and saves His people. In her simple decision of faith, she willingly surrendered everything she had to His mercy!

This is why Rahab's faith was honored so much in the New Testament. The Lord and His apostles recognize it as a very excellent example of the kind of faith that moves the heart of God.

It remains so today. When a person surrenders everything, places all their hope in Him, and even their lives on earth as well as in eternity, then, they discover that God transforms them and supplies them with the ability to trust Him with any problem, or need. Suddenly, they possess the kind of faith that can move mountains.

Faith is vitally important in the life of the Christian. It is by faith that you are saved; you are justified; cleansed, preserved, blessed and look forward to the return of Jesus. Faith is where you please God, admit your dependence upon Him and your faithfulness to Him, and continually seek to rely upon Him and His grace. It is a faith like Rahab's.

Faith transformed Rahab's life and household in a far more significant way than any vase could transform a room.

Chapter 6

Shadrach, Meshach, and Abednego: Faithful Men Aflame

"Faith means, whether I am visibly delivered or not, I will stick to my belief that God is love. There are some things only learned in a fiery furnace." Oswald Chambers.

Part One: The Story behind the Lesson

If you ask any child in Sunday school, which stories they remember and you will hear a shout for "Daniel and the Fiery Furnace. Stories from the Book of Daniel connect with children, and the one starring Daniel's three comrades is no exception. It is a perfect expose of future events blended with real life drama of people modeling the type of faith to survive the worst possible prophetic events.

Our first glimpse of these three people is in chapter two where, together with Daniel, they face a death sentence for daring to obey the Word's requirement for their lifestyle. In this chapter, Daniel is conspicuously absent; but Shadrach, Mesach, and Abednego stand as firm in their faith as they did in chapter two.

Prophecy is an important aspect of the Bible because it provides empirical evidence to support the dogmatic truth regarding the nature of God, and how to know Him personally. So much of the prophecies in Daniel have already come to pass, that the few remaining events are considered to be completely trustworthy. Perhaps the strength of prophecy's believability lies, in part, in the way in which the people whose lives are intertwined in its presentation were people of extraordinary character and faith. Their action enhanced the trustworthiness of their words.

Today our world is embroiled in the playing out of the very events that Daniel prophesied. So a fresh look at the type of faith required surviving, and even succeeding in the midst of such turmoil. In Daniel I see two principles revealed. The first: Until one can walk by faith today, surviving tomorrow will be impossible. The second: the truth of the Bible is meant to be understood not with intellect alone, but also with the heart.

The Book divides into two main divisions. The first section (Chapter 1-6) describes the personal lives of Daniel and his three Jewish companions in Babylon. These four men lived by faith in the true and living God in the midst of pagan idolatry and hostile political pressure. Their faithfulness was significantly rewarded with every kind of blessing. For the three men we now seek to learn about faith from, the blessing came from a very fiery trial.

If you are employed in a workplace that is dominated by those who take God's name in vain, and ridicule people of faith, then you can find no more counsel and encouragement than in reading of the experiences of these four men in this Book

If you are a teenager or a college student you will find your heart stirred as you learn that these young people, hauled off in chains to walk four hundred miles to begin a life under the thumb of a ruthless dictator. Also, they had to face each new trial without benefit of older mentors—only their knowledge of the Word and their trust in the Lord to guide them each day. Theirs was a daily existence in a very hostile environment.

Background to the Furnace

Perhaps you are familiar with their first trial. It is described in Daniel chapter two. From childhood, they had been told by God what they were not to eat, and the most powerful tyrant on earth, a man known for ruthless torture, was telling them that unless they ate exactly what God had forbidden, they would die. It is a true test of faith: comply with Nebuchadnezzar's demand or be executed.

No doubt friends urged them to "go along to get along". "Don't lose your life over food". But they saw it as an opportunity to stand firm in their faith, and God surely honored them. As a result, they are promoted to jobs of prominence.

On the heels of this test, their success placed them in the place of their next test. Actually, that still occurs. People of faith are ever being pressed by the pressures of this world system to cave into to the temptations at every turn of the trail of life. Such tests provide opportunities for true believers to demonstrate their faithfulness. Also, such tests provide an opportunity for God to bless the world about us, including the most powerful who often embrace the idea that God either does not exist, or has no interest in man, nor is capable of impacting any real life situation. Such trials provide opportunities for people of faith to demonstrate to this watching world that God not only exists, but He is actively involved in the affairs or people, and He is a force to be reckoned with.

Fiery Furnace

Nebuchadnezzar had listened to Daniel's interpretation of the Image in his explanation of the Image with Head of Gold, chest of silver, thighs of Brass, and Feet of Iron and Clay. He was told that his kingdom represented the Head of Gold. Nebuchadnezzar then set about to build a replica of this and use it as a loyalty test to strengthen his power by having all the people in top management under his control to assemble and bow down to it. The success of the three comrades put them in this crowd. Why Daniel was not present we are not told.

To encourage everyone to express their devotion, the king assembled a very impressive orchestra to create a sense of carnival, and a raging fiery furnace to motivate the reluctant. Everybody complied except our three friends with the strange sounding names.

You can imagine how they were yanked before the king and ordered to comply. In this moment they proved they were people of pure faith.

They addressed the crowd with the king before them and the heat radiating behind them. They shared, with quiet solemnity that they had made up their minds so that not even he could change their decision.

They admitted that their God could deliver them from the fiery furnace, but whether He chose to do this or not, that decision remained His to make. Their task was to remain faithful to Him. Notice their words of great trust: "they speak words of great faith: "Our God is able to, but we don't know the mind of God. His thoughts are greater than our thoughts. His ways are different from ours. It may be that he won't do it. But even if he doesn't, (we will remain faithful to Him)" (3:18)

By this statement they demonstrated that they had learned that there are things more important than physical life. They staked their lives on remaining faithful even at the risk of death. Yet, in their statement you see that they knew that in trusting God, they were entering into the zone of perfect favor—more blessed than even Nebuchadnezzar could bestow on them. Part of the reasoning behind a decision to trust God alone, is the knowledge that God will not be in any man's debt, so He will greatly honor any demonstration of faith.

Suddenly, bound hand and foot, they were tossed into a furnace so incredibly hot that the people throwing them into it perished in the heat.

Then the work of faith began to show the watching world who really rules it. There were suddenly four in the furnace and the other looked like the Son of Man. Shortly, thereafter, they walked out, perhaps stepping over the smoldering carcasses of their executioners. And all marveled that they bore no evidence of having ever been out in the sun let alone inside a furnace. The world discovered the power of trusting as it witnessed the fact that not even their clothes had the odor of smoke.

That confrontation between people of faith and a system of works resulted in the king who ordered them into the furnace, entered into a kind of furnace where he wandered for several years tormented by the flames of psychological madness. Finally, as He had the three trusting Hebrews, God brought Nebuchadnezzar back to sanity. As was their testimony, so the king gave tribute to the Lord:

Shadrach, Meshach, and Abednego: Faithful Men Aflame

"Now I, Nebuchadnezzar, praise, extol and honor the King of heaven; for all his works are right and his ways are just; and those who walk in pride he is able to abase." {Dan 4:37}.

No doubt the actions of Daniel as well as the three friends of the fiery furnace were instrumental in God capturing the heart of the most powerful despot, ruling the greatest empire in history.

As I reflect on this, two ideas emerged. First, how many dictators—Genghis Khan, Stalin, Mao Tse-tung, etc., have asserted themselves as solo players, not realizing that they were, in fact, only playing a part that has been prophetically composed for them. Sadly, these types never understand the fact that God alone remains in command. So it remains for people of faith to demonstrate this by standing firm against the power of such tyrants.

Second, how God, no matter how evil and awful life gets, ever seeks to honor the trusting obedience of those who lay their faith and their lives on the line in a way to honor Him and His word with trusting obedience. The events of this fiery furnace prove that God who has power over every aspect of life and death, remains ever eager to reach down to honor our efforts to genuinely trust Him by turning His power toward our needs, to listen to our questions, and problems and move to unravel the messes that our faith prompts. Truly, if anything, this proves that he is the God worth trusting.

Part Two: Learning from Them

Shadrach, Meshach, and Abednego discovered that it is not easy to live out one's faith in a society that emphasizes and glorifies the secular and the sensational. They found themselves being pressured to bow down to gods of gold and silver, to be in awe of man's intellect and power. Yet, they refused to compromise their faith! Not much has changed in 2,500 years! The struggle at a societal level between people living by faith and people living by works and wits remains the same now as in Babylon.

The gods of gold and silver have a slightly different shape (pieces of paper and metal coinage now!) but they are still worshipped and people still "sacrifice" important things to them like their families and their faith!

The 90-foot image of a man that Nebuchadnezzar constructed as a way of affirming his power and striking awe and worship in those that beheld it is not much different than the monument men build today to obtain power and fame and fortune.

So what else is new? Is it so different today? Isn't this just what our society is teaching our young people still? To bow to the god of humanism, coated with the god of mammon (money) and taught that it is a good thing to adulate to those they perceive as possessing "star" power?

In this postmodern era, man is taught to glory in man's universal, sovereign power, and to revere the idea of doing it all without any interference from the Almighty. The primary focus of the multitude is to figure new and easier ways of making more money and capturing a position higher up on the power ladder of power. Today, young people face great pressures to compromise their faith in God and go along with the world's ideas.

Likewise, in this modern era, we can easily find ourselves in a situation where spiritual principles take a back seat to one's occupation and busy lifestyle? The ugly reality is that if one gives into these pressures, perhaps, then, this is the time for one to consider this question: "Have I not begun to bow the knee to a mighty statue also?

Ironically, their recent promotion of high political office set the trap for Shadrach, Meshach, and Abednego. It had brought them to this fiery furnace. It just had not yet been lit. One can imagine that in the act of such an immoral choice they might have rationalized:

- "We know it isn't a real god, so it won't mean anything to us if we just bow; In fact, it will keep the peace so we can continue our ministry." or,
- "If we bow this one time we at least will have an opportunity to share our faith later with all these ungodly people." or,
- "If we don't bow and are killed, who will be here to witness to all these people?"

No matter how well meaning such statements might be, such action would have been a compromise of faith.

Also, it is probably fair to say that Nebuchadnezzar was probably ignorant about the theological consequences of his edict—he had no desire to tangle with the God of Israel—he saw this as an important loyalty oath.

But his ignorance, nevertheless, did not excuse those who did understand the theological consequences from ignoring the true issues. All he was seeking was for them to publicly confess that their love and faith in the King of Kings would not interfere with their devotion and loyalty to him.

The three Hebrews saw this as a compromise of their relationship with God. So they ignored the command to bow down, and then told him to his face that their actions were based on their faith in God who was, in contrast to Nebuchadnezzar:

- Was capable of doing anything He pleases, even to save them from the furnace
- Did not have to deliver them to be worthy of their trust;
- Trusting Him would free them from the King's power.

What a testimony to the eternal God before this temporal king.

Thank God for these three men who refused to compromise their faith in God in order to bow to these pressures from the ungodly society they lived and worked in, this means we can learn from their example.

Without their example we would never have received such a dramatic proof of God's willingness to back up His promises to care for those who choose to live by faith in His Word, even at risk of life.

God does not promise to keep us FROM the fires when we are faithful to Him, but He does promise to be with us IN the fire! So this episode recorded in the third chapter of Daniel enables us to discover principles to bless our faith.

That seems to be practical lesson number one.

Practical Lesson Number Two

Perhaps, after probing into the lives of these Godly models, it is appropriate for us to pause and share some of our own personal observations regarding faith.

1. The faith process begins with me, as I personally take the initiative to search out God's promises and develop my faith with His cultivation. In this regard, permit me to make these observations:

- Faith originates with God and is appropriated by prayer. The apostles recognized this and prayed, "Lord increase our faith".
- Since it is one of the fruit of the Spirit (Galatians 5:22), by asking the Holy Spirit to take total control of our lives, we are, in effect, appropriating faith.

2. Biblical faith releases a higher law than the law of nature even though nature declares the handiwork of God. I need to start from the Scriptures with a specific word or promise from God to transcend His natural laws. His promises become my assurance.

3. All faith begins as a "gift of faith" (1 Corinthians 12). Think of faith as a seed that is planted. Then it grows as I cultivate it through meditation and prayer which releases the Holy Spirit's nurturing power. How does this process work? Permit me to offer these suggestions:
- I meditate by continuously ruminating on His word by thinking, speaking and confessing the same thing over and over to God and myself. The Holy Spirit's illumination causes me to "see" deep spiritual riches in His promises (Eph. 1:17-18). Then I discover ways, in my every day experiences, to act upon the truth the Holy Spirit reveals to me. As I seek to honor Him by applying his Word, I discover a peaceful assurance within my soul that God is pleased with my actions.
- I also seek in every situation to release greater and greater levels of faith in order to please God and receive answers from Him. Because of my level of trust in God that is continually increasing by virtue of an ongoing personal relationship, based on trusting and obeying His Word. This occurs as I act in faith in every circumstance to do what He commands me. I also confess the truth over the situation. I can testify, dear reader, that over the years of this pattern, that God has blessed my life, my family, and my ministry incredibly—as He will bless you for applying these same principles.

Even though we have each received our measured out portion of faith, as described in (Romans 12:3), nevertheless, one must never think that this negates the promise that each of us can progress from a state of small faith to that of a "great faith".

4. Biblical faith is the daring of the soul to go farther than it can see. It is not just blind to impossibilities, it is also deaf to doubt, and dumb to discouragement. It knows nothing but success in God. This faith is taking God at His word (Mark 11:22) as its object instead of being based upon religious feelings or kind intentions.

5. In facing life's problems, trusting faith serves as a shield by which we can ask God to provide a covering over our souls in times of danger, as the friends of Daniel did.

6. Faith results from facing our failure by repentance. In the Holy Spirit's work to restore us to fellowship, our faith is suddenly stimulated within us to trust Him, because we, in repentance, we recognize our inability to trust Him, and ask Him for a fresh gift of faith, and immediately place it in His will and Word.

7. Faith alone makes victorious daily living possible (1 John 5:4). It is the defining quality that enables a saved man to live—the just shall live by faith" (Romans 1:17). This faith in God and His Word is the transforming agent to bring us into the image of Christ. The Bible is the mind of Christ and we are commanded to think with the mind of Christ (Phil. 2:5). Since victorious living is the result of faith, we must take care that we try to live otherwise (through shortcuts and substitute assurance). As you can see, the more we conform to the image of Christ, the more victorious our lives will be.

8. Faith is the most powerful force in the world- (Mark 11:22-23). Jesus speaking figuratively of the power of faith, sought to teach His disciples (and us) that a mountain (the largest possible physical obstacle in nature) could not prevent a divine promise for its movement to be executed. Any and all human obstacles retreat when confronted with biblical faith because it will direct God's power at the obstacle and certainly the obstacle will obey.

9. Faith is belief in action (Heb.11:4-7, 8). James wrote that a passive faith is not biblical faith - (2:14-20). He said that if one's faith does not produce good works, it must be considered as dead faith. This is the kind

of faith that the Holy Spirit implants in the trusting heart; and it always produces good works (actions).

10. Faith validates our hope for the future - (Hebrews 11:1) by making heaven real, as well as removing doubts, and hesitations, since the eye of faith is able to see more clearly than the physical eye could.

Conclusion

Ah, dear reader, my prayer is that these principles from the lives of Shadrach, Meshach, and Abednego will help you how to respond, by faith, under pressure from the next fiery trial you may be thrown into.

I have shared practical principles, which I have learned by experience by walking by faith over decades.

I have shared them with the desire that they should serve as a catalyst in aiding you to recall even more principles from your own personal quest to become a person who truly walks by faith.

So, the next time life heats up a cauldron of trouble and attempts to destroy you by dumping you into such a fiery trial, I pray that you will turn to the lessons learned from these three friends of Daniel.

Now, we are ready to investigate a man on whom a mountain of trouble fell upon, and how his experience can provide us insights into how to move this load of rock and debris off our life. We will now listen to the woeful experience of a man who was a contemporary of Abraham, a Gentile, and a true man of faith—that was sorely tested—Job.

Chapter 7

Faith to Survive a Mountain Falling on You

Reflections on Job

You would be amazed at the Bible scholars who insist that Job was not a real man, but rather a fictitious character starring in a mythological poem. Truth is, he was a very real person who was a contemporary of Abraham, and a prominent citizen in a nearby city.

The prophet Ezekiel said that he considered Job to be one of the three great men of the Old Testament, alongside Noah and Daniel (Ezekiel 14:14, 20). James, the Apostle, also held Job up as a model of patience and steadfast endurance.

Dr. Francis Schaeffer wrote that the first argument of the Gospel is not that Jesus died for our sins, but that "God is there (exists), and He is not silent, i.e., is in control of human history.

Amazingly, this Book deals with this very issue by pointing out that through human suffering, God not only deals with the problem, but, simultaneously uses the healing process to strengthen His relationship with the sufferer. So this oldest Book in the Bible tackles one of the most current issues—where is God when you hurt.

Another amazing thing about this book: it features a Gentile, a contemporary of Abraham, with a very vibrant faith, and enough accurate theological understanding that he could argue doctrine. Since Abraham is the father of our faith, Job's understanding is remarkable. I think it proves that God is able to reveal Himself to whomever He chooses.

I love the way the message of this Book unfolds. It begins with a description of a man with a strong faith, and idyllic life. Then he becomes the focal point for a fight between God and Satan. The Devil accuses God of cuddling those who express their faith in Him, with this speech: "Man trusts You because of the blessings that he gets from You. Without these benefits, nobody would trust you; but would curse you and backslide."

God replied that this contention was not true. People, like Job, for example, serve and trust Me with no regard to a *quid pro quo* payback.

Satan then argued, "Give me Job and I will prove my point.

God agrees, but not to allow Satan to take his life. With this brief background, we will now present the message of the Book.

Part One: Understanding the Message of Job

Job was a highly respected, prosperous national figure. But, in response to Satanic attack, in a matter of a few days, his world collapsed on his head. Natural disasters and criminals destroyed his financial world, and then his children were all killed while meeting to celebrate with a meal.

Suddenly overwhelmed by misery, Job begins to wonder: "What on earth is the purpose of my life since it is now filled with such anguish? Everything I had is gone, and everyone I loved is dead. I feel like ending my life and going home to heaven."

Fortunately, he lived. For us, the result was a blessed insight into the problem of suffering, and where is God when you are hurting in the midst of that suffering. For him, the lesson had a happy ending—his fortune was restored, and he gained a new family twice the size of the one that died.

What is so fascinating about these insights is that this issue continues today by the forces of evil that insist on blaming God for suffering in the world (which is due to the Evil One). So Job's message can be so helpful to anyone who faces suffering trials. As I share it with you, dear reader, my prayer is that you will gain hope and insights into how to pray and trust the Lord when you need to exercise the kind of faith that can move a mountain that has just fallen upon your head.

We have laid out the background and essential premise of this story. But the argument that leads the reader to the right answers concerning suffering and God's role in the midst of it all was carried along by four "friends", Eliphaz, Bildad, Zophar, and Elihu who showed up to minister to him in his pain. Three of them hammered him with bad theology and blaming accusations. Elihu remained the exception. But, from their bad doctrine, we learn valuable lessons into the kind of faith required to survive trials of the magnitude of Job's.

Eliphaz

Eliphas was the first to speak; he said to Job, "C'mon, you've helped others with this same kind of spiritual problem, so now it is your turn to follow your own counsel and you will be relieved from the pain". Then, he points out the source of Job's problem: God never punishes the righteous; so Job's situation was due to his own willful disobedience. Eliphaz concluded, "Job, if you will recognize that this mess occurred in your life because of some un-confessed sin in your life, and, now, confess, and repent, and you will find healing and deliverance.

Eliphaz is the type who sees the LORD as the God of Justice, but chooses to ignore God's mercy, loving kindness, and grace etc.). His theology is true, but shortsighted. I would be inclined to buy Eliphaz's ideas; except, I have ministered long enough to have observed many Godly people whose walks were free from unconfessed sin in their lives, yet, suffered terribly.

But, thanks to Eliphaz, we learn one of the reasons for the Book—to show that suffering CAN have nothing to do with judgment, and it carries a deeper reason for its terrible pain than just punishing sinners. To appreciate this, observe Job's response to Eliphaz.

Job replies: "If there is something wrong in my life, I am not aware of it. True, I do know that this tragedy has befallen me by the Hand of God; I just don't know why. Since I know that I have no unconfessed sin in my life, I am convinced that Eliphaz's reasoning is wrong".

Then, unfortunately, Job then makes the wrong argument about his condition. Instead of trying to find out God's purpose for his calamity, Job begins to whine and complain to God that his suffering is too unbearable.

Center of the War

Before we proceed further to understand the message of this Book, let us focus on the issues in the conflict as they impact the forces of heaven and those of hell.

Job is the focal point of two large imposing spiritual forces. On the one hand there is the army of the evil One. Satan's purpose is to use pain to weary him physically, misguided compassion of his friends to irritate his soul, and the silence of the Lord to pound Job's spirit into unconsciousness — and all in an effort to break the man's faith.

On the other hand, God has His purpose in Job's suffering:
- To use pain to teach Job new insights into faith and in relating to Him;
- To help Job understand the purpose for suffering;
- To prove Satan wrong as to his accusations about why people trust God; and,
- To demonstrate to the watching world that no matter how little you understand what is happening to your life, God is worth trusting because He knows best what He is doing.

Now, dear reader, you have a glimpse into the deep truth Job can teach you about the meaning of true faith. With this in mind, let us return to the pursuit of an understanding of the meaning of this important Book.

Bildad's Prickly Counsel

Friend number two, Bildad, approached Job, in the midst of his suffering with his own special tactic. Rather than take Eliphaz's finger-pointing approach, he chose to slice the man's heart with the following cold-blooded logic:
1. God can do no wrong

2. God punishes all wrong; therefore any tragedy is the result of some definite and perhaps hidden sin.
3. God will respond to repentance, because it is His nature to bless those who turn to him, and that he rebukes and punishes those who turn away.
4. Man, by nature, must have God's blessing in order to prosper. If he lacks it, he had to have done something to cut himself off from God's blessing, so repent.

What's wrong with this man's argument? He is attempting to analyze a spiritual condition with a logical solution.

Problems with the Counsel of both Men

While their counsel contained good theology, it failed because of the following factors:

1. It lacked sufficient empathy to make them credible. No one listens to someone unless they perceive him or her to be genuinely concerned and seeking to help. Their words belie no desire to understand Job's pain or complaint.
2. Their argument was theologically, built around only one of God's attributes—His justice. Attributes more appropriate to dealing with suffering would be Mercy, Loving Kindness, etc. As a result of their doctrinal blindness they failed to consider that his suffering might be due to something other than sin.
3. Notice that they failed to mention that they had prayed for guidance before they spoke. Without intercession, there can be no illumination about how to speak encouragement to a hurting heart.
4. They chose to be seen as orthodox, rather than caring. This attitude (selfishness) belies an uncleanness that always distorts godliness and helps no one. Pharisees practiced this; in the day Jesus faced it. Think of Eliphaz as the type of Pharisee that uses "nice guy, warm sounding platitudes to put Job in his place. While Bildad resembles another type of Pharisee that thinks he has conceived the perfectly logical reason for everything. And Zophar, he is the man who will substitute "heat" (impassioned arguing) for "light"

(insightful reasons that makes good sense) as an approach to "helping" Job.
5. All of these people placed God in a box: they felt that they so completely understood the Lord that they were able to predict how He would always act and explain why. Therefore, when they encounter a situation, like Job's, they revert to giving out "pat answers" that fit the picture of God they have in their boxes.

Someone has said that there are only two kinds of speakers: those who have something to say, and those who have to say something. Job's three friends are the latter kind, and they kept a dialogue going until it has finally ground to a halt.

Job's Transformation

In spite of these clowns, Job's own attitude does begin to change. The change can be tracked along these two milestones.

First, midway into the drama Job admits, "Let's assume that you are correct; that I *am* in this mess because of my sin. It is true that I cannot imagine what that would be since I have always been careful to deal with all of my sins by repentance. So, although I cannot prove that you have wrongly accused me; I'm not ready to concede that you have rightly accused me, either. However, I am open to being convinced from the Word that you are right. So, accomplish that and I will take your counsel and act accordingly.

Next, Job cries out for some insight from the Lord. In answer to his prayer, a new man, Elihu, enters the fray. He offers counsel that mirrors the mind of the Lord. Job recognizes this answer to his prayer and views the counsel as from the throne of God.

Enter Elihu

Two important clues helped Job listen to him. His name meant, "My God is he", also, he was the son of Barachel, meaning, "God blesses." Job knew these things because the man came from a nearby region known as Buz. Truly, Elihu's approach was a breath of fresh air.

After sitting, silently, throughout the ongoing arguments of the other three (who managed to make matters worse) Elihu suddenly feels compelled to share an insight that God had given him, rather than offer another personal opinion. Also, his approach, in contrast to the caustic statements of the other three men, is marked by courtesy and sensitivity that showed that he genuinely recognized the depth of Job's suffering. Finally, he saw his role as a mediator, to bring understanding between Job and the three "Pharisees".

Elihu's counsel bears this silent testimony that God agreed with it: at the conclusion of the Book, when the Lord rebukes the three others, Elihu is excluded from any criticism.

Elihu's Arguments:

1. There is a presence in our pains of a mediator. It is God, who in the midst of our sufferings teaches us that He is working out purposes that we do not understand but are for our good.
2. This God helps us to see that in love He is training us, steadying us, and teaching us through the time of stress," (Romans 5:3-4).
3. When the mediator speaks to us through the suffering, we see the blessing in it.
4. Without His comforting insights, human suffering produces bitterness, resentment, anger, frustration, revolt and rebellion against God's will.
5. Solving this type of problem requires a mediator (not just a reference to a counselor, but a reference to a future Messiah, the ultimate Mediator).

As a result of Elihu's comments, Job suddenly begins to understand something about his situation that he had never known before: He sees that if he allows that mediator's work to guide him through this time, he shall be restored.

Now Elihu launches into his mediator work. To start the process, he summarizes Job's view of God, and with empathy for Job's argument:

- If we behave ourselves, God ought to give us blessing and prosperity.

- I did all of this, so God has treated me in an unjust manner, and on top of all that, He is unwilling to enlighten me as to why this entire calamity has fallen on me.
- "What advantage is it to me to behave myself? I might just as well have sinned." Now, with this as a background, I will begin to answer Job's complaints.

Next, Elihu begins to analyze Job's words.

Elihu's Analysis of Job's Complaints

First, Elihu says, "Job your complaint mirrors that of the ungodly. Such feelings demonstrate an ignorance of the true understanding of God's character and nature.

Elihu's True Assessment of God in Midst of Suffering

Then Elihu shares insights about God, can help change one's attitude toward suffering:
- God cannot be unjust. Therefore, no matter how long it may take, God is going to treat the wicked with judgment and bless the righteous; because, to do otherwise would make God unjust.
- Being sovereign, and the originator of all things, God is beyond accountability to man.
- The only true sense of justice on this earth is obtained from God Himself—He invented the concept; whatever we know of the meaning of this word, we learn from Him.
- Since God knows everything, He is capable of knowing exactly what every human heart is feeling and each mind thinks.
- Questioning His decisions is nonsense because they are all based on impeccable logic and totally consistent with all revealed truth
- God is not interested in reform, He only seeks repentance, and surrender of the right to run your life, that is what he is after, and he will accept no other basis for relationship with Him.
- God's problem with Job is that the man spoke out of an ignorance of His true nature and character.

- God chose to use suffering to bring Job to the truth; hence it must continue until Job fully understood the point of it all.
- Job is a righteous, good man, and sincerely seeks to serve God. But his thinking is flawed in that he feels he can do it through his own efforts—by behaving himself in obedience to the Truth he possesses to achieve righteousness as he perceives it.
- All human righteousness is as filthy rags in God's sight, so man can only be righteous by accepting what God has said by this gift of righteousness—not by trying to conceive self-efforts in the hope of manufacturing righteousness.
- God's ways are not intended to be directed at you with anger or malice.
- In dealing with suffering, God may appear (by His silence) to be indifferent to your cry for help. But this is due to one or both of the following reasons: i) the timing of the lesson is not complete; or ii) the cry is for relief and not repentance.

What a sharp contrast to the counter-productive palaver of the other three "friends".

Perhaps this is the lesson of the book: Man, in the midst of his suffering fails to see God's larger purpose in it for one or more of the following reasons:

i) He wants to gain the attention of the sufferer in order to speak to him and build a closer relationship;

ii) God wants to use the suffering to demonstrate to the watching world the power of grace (so others may be saved through the sufferer's experience.

iii) God desires to expose Satan's philosophy of suffering (that it happens to people who deserve it) as a way of smashing the head of the Serpent.

Finally, Elihu asks Job to consider two things. First, he invites Job to focus on how glorious God truly is. He is beyond men's ability to understand Him. He operates differently than men do. He also uses His powers for both blessing and judgment alike.

Second, Elihu ask Job to try and appreciate that God has many reasons for doing as He chooses to do, and that His reasons are inscrutable, and realize that if Job truly wants to know why He visits us with affliction or adversity, then Job must come to him with a contrite humility asking Him to explain His purpose.

Conclusion to Part One

I find it amazing that Job and these people, in such a primitive time held such an understanding of the true God, and true faith, that they could attempt to speak to such a complex human need such as suffering. There can only be one reason for this depth of knowledge.

They learned it from the descendants of Noah who preached a Gospel based on the words of God to Adam, Eve, and Satan in the Garden after their sin. (Genesis 3:14-19). It captured the entire plan of salvation in a nutshell. With it, man could know God and how to live by faith. These people had heard this Gospel presentation and embraced the One it proclaimed. (More on this shortly).

Abraham's unique calling was to become the father of the chosen people, and set up the lineage of the Messiah. He was not the first man to believe God. He was just the father of the Messianic faith.

Now that we have accomplished this analysis of the Message of this Book, we will now seek to understand how to exercise sufficient faith to remove a mountain that has fallen upon us.

Part Two: What Job can teach us About True Faith

For so many reasons, the Book of Job provides extraordinary insights about faith. Permit me to share these more important ones.

1. True Faith was Understood and Possessed by Men from Adam to Abraham

In that fateful moment after their Sin in the Garden, God pronounces a very important prophecy (Gen. 3:14 -19). Theologians call this the "Protoevangelium". Think of it as the Gospel in Miniature because its four themes become the substance of every Book thereafter unto Revelation. These themes are:
- the nature of evil, and its source, Satan;
- the nature of the Kingdom and its ultimate triumph;

- the nature of the people who inhabit the Kingdom, called people who possess the life of the Son of God; and
- the nature of the Seed, the One called God the Son as central to human history.

From history we know that this "Pre-Flood Gospel" was preached throughout the world using certain signs (not astrological signs!) to use the stars of the night sky as visual aids for forty-eight messages covering every aspect of these four themes.

Historians have discovered that Shem developed the preaching system, and Abraham taught it to a group of people who preserved it into the time of Jesus' birth and used it to find His birthplace. They were called "the Wise Men".

After the Flood, the descendants of Noah continued to evangelize the world. From this ministry we have men like Job, non-Semites who were contemporaries of Abraham, but who were not to be included in the covenant ministry that would lead to Jesus and to the true Believers of the 21st century. Perhaps you are thinking, "Yeah? But, is this the kind of faith I possess as a Christian?" Absolutely, because true faith, i.e., as evidenced in the dialogue of Job is the very kind God accepts. As proof, Job confesses that his trust in Jehovah (Old Testament Jesus) would qualify him for the resurrection of the saints.

This is why God could teach Job and his friends the difference between a faith that will work during sunny days and clear sailing, vs. the kind that can sustain you when the mountain falls on your head.

When you think about it, this all makes very good sense. As soon as God created man, His first desire was to establish a personal relationship with Him. The only kind of fellowship He could tolerate would be with people who would act with integrity, and that required trust. So we should not be surprised to learn that faith is not a Christian thing. True, the New Testament validated the message God taught Shem, as well as Abraham; even amplified its meaning. But these people lacked nothing of the essential nature of true Biblical faith

2. Genuine Faith Handles Real World Messes

The kind of faith that God designed and demanded for a meaningful relationship, deals with life as it really exists, not mythical belief systems. Review the religious ideas of creation to Job's generation and you will hear stories like this "The world was hatched from an egg (by a mammal) and remains stable because it is supported on the backs of four giant turtles".

What a contrast with what you hear from these men of this Book. Their faith was built on dogmatic truth, as well as the empirical evidence based on Noah's prophecy of the Flood and its occurrence. Therefore, it was like our own Biblical faith.

Notice that the Book revealed life where the ordinary is impacted by the supernatural; and problems often have a spiritual dimension. Bad things actually happen because of Satan's influence. Good things happen as a result of God's grace and mercy. Job—like us—gets into such messes because of the conflict between good and evil, and this will continue until the Messiah crushes the head of Satan (Rev. 19)

Thanks to the Book of Job, we gain an understanding of the true nature of evil"

- It is not just the sins of murder, and immorality, but also includes such subtle sins as selfishness. The root cause of all sin is human pride.
- Suffering does not just happen to people who sin; it can happen to people who live a stellar example of trusting obedience. God has larger purposes for doing what He does, such as revealing His glory, and bringing people to repentance through the testimony of the godly sufferer.
- Satan has real power in this world; therefore, he is constantly causing bad things to happen to good people.

So the Book is most informative for what it teaches us about faith in a real world with real supernatural forces colliding over the heads of mortals who sincerely seek to honor the Lord but ended up in the same "boat" as Job.

Faith to Survive a Mountain Falling On You

3. True Faith Is Sufficient for Bad Times as well as Good

We have discussed Job's early concept of the faith life: do right and God will reward you with a trouble free existence.

Likewise, we saw how his friends, convinced that his calamity proved that the man practiced, in secret, deep forms of evil, and therefore, if he would repent would find the mountain of debris miraculously begin to fly away from atop him.

But the purpose for the Book was to teach us valuable things about how genuine faith can sustain a trusting heart in the midst of a terrible life tragedy. All insights stem from this central one: Trusting God will not enable anyone to enjoy a trouble free existence. From this main idea, we learn these other truths about how God views a person trusting Him:

- God has a purpose for your life that is larger than just providing you a comfortable existence.
- Just because God loves you deeply, you are not immune from going into rough waters if it fulfills His purpose (as was the case of His own Son);
- Often, God's most faithful followers prove the steadfastness of their faith as they go through such rough waters—which happened because of no unbelief or rebellion on their part. This occurs because His ways are not our ways.
- The only way to face tribulations with true faith is to approach it with the attitude Job developed: "I have no idea why this has happened to me. If someone can show me an area of sin in my life that I need to repent of, I will gladly do so. Meanwhile, I choose to trust Him in spite of not knowing why this is happening to me—even if I lose my life.

4. The Nature of True Faith

At the outset, Job thought he was exercising true faith when he obeyed God and did what was right when he considered it in his best interest to do so.

He typifies those sincere people who live their daily lives by assuming that they are exercising great faith when they believe that God is there;

He is watching, therefore they need to do the right thing because if they fail in this regard, they will suffer the consequences.

Do not misunderstand; such people are practicing a kind of faith in the Lord. But it is more about following a code and embracing a lifestyle than building a personal relationship with the Lord. As a result, without this unique personal, vital, ongoing connection, their faith remains weak. As a result, when a deep personal problem occurs, "fair weather" faith turns to faithless worry. Such unbelief can befall anyone—even people in the worst of circumstances, even in an environment where faith was tested daily. Permit me to illustrate.

I read about a small group of true believers, decades ago, attempting to quietly hold a prayer meeting in Russia when it was completely illegal to do so. To protect themselves they devised a complex plan.

Prior to the meeting, individuals would drift into the meeting house over a six hour period hoping to fool the neighbors and the police and not be arrested for congregating.

Suddenly after they began to worship, the knock on the front door told them they were in serious trouble; facing long jail sentences. In strode two policemen, guns drawn. The first one yells, "If you do not want to die for your faith, better run for your lives". Like scared rabbits, a few jumped up and ran. The second one echoed the command, "If you don't want to die in prison for your Jesus you better leave immediately. Would you believe that about one fourth of the assembly exited the meeting?

The cops stood there in silence for about ten minutes. Finally the first one said, "Sorry about that. We are policemen and we were sent to arrest Believers in Jesus. But last week we were converted by the people we attempted to arrest, and now we are followers of Him also. We devised this plan because any Christian willing to die for his faith will not turn us into the authorities."

True faith does not fear, in the midst of the worst of circumstances; rather, it stands firm.

Job had to learn this. At first, he was a man thoroughly defeated. He lost all his children and grandchildren, property, and possessions in a few days. Then his own wife turned against him. He was confused, crushed, and felt betrayed by the Lord he had tried to serve. But after the boils befell him, and the three friends hammered on him, he spiraled into a deep level of misery. Eventually, he started to get the true picture. Suddenly, he told his critics, "No matter what, I will trust Him—even if it kills me. So what, death will be my transport into His presence". That is true faith.

What was the difference? His initial faith included trust, it rested mainly on his own confidence that his efforts would garner him favor with God. This cannot be, since all human efforts to please God are "as filthy rags".

There can be no trust mingled with the leaven of "I do my best; maintain a lifestyle that pleases Him, so He will not allow any bad things to befall me or my family". Not true!

You might recall that this was the very argument that Satan laid before God, "Job trust and serves You because you take care of him. If you remove your hand of blessing from him, he'll curse you to your face," {Job 1:11}. In this he was half correct.

Many people are living like this. They are really only serving God as long as he blesses them. As soon as adversity appears at the threshold of their life, they want to quit trusting and serving Him. They turn their back on what they had professed about their Christian faith and thrown it all over and were living for themselves and for the world. It is weak faith that only serves God when he blesses.

But thank God, Job came to see the nature of true faith. He realized that genuine faith relies on no human confidence; and it becomes most evident when one is going through a most difficult situation. Also, he had the benefit of a man sent from God to bring clarity to all. Elihu was able to guide Job to trust the Lord amid his own trembling failure by getting him to cling in helplessness to God and humbly invite the Lord to explain what all the suffering meant, in order to strengthen Job's faith in the Lord. That is why Job becomes an example of faith.

Job's true faith is the same kind that Jesus, in Gethsemane exhibited. Facing the threat of premature physical death by Satan, before He could accomplish His work on the Cross, His humanity became overcome with fear of failure. But, immediately, His faith took over his thinking and He prayed, "Ah Father, in spite of the fact that I do not know all that lies ahead, nevertheless, I trust You implicitly—Your will be done! {Matt 26:39}.

So Job teaches us another principle about faith: Great faith is usually being exercised when you least feel like you are being faithful; when you are so weak, helpless and desperate that you can do nothing but simply cling to the Lord and His promises.

5. True faith sees the Larger Picture in which a calamity exists.

It is about more than just the events that have befallen us or our families, financial security, or health; because behind it all, and integral to it all, a battle rages that draws the full force of evil against the forces of heaven. Because, as a true Believer, you share the very nature of Christ, and Satan hates Him and seeks in every way to hurt Him.

As a Christian, you possess the Spirit of God, therefore, Satan sees Him within you, and this automatically makes you a target for his evil attacks. And this is why suffering exists.

What Job learned about the Nature of true Faith that genuinely pleases God, and moves Him to answer our prayers can be summarized as follows:

True Faith Relies on Nothing Human
He learned that true faith must not rely on any human resources. In fact, true faith shines when we have no resources to stand on. In this deep experience we discover another principle of faith: our weakness becomes our only resource. On the other hand, bad faith always feels comforted by secretly holding other options.

True Faith Never Seeks to Share God's Glory
Job learned that human natures longs to share the glory of God, serve Him in order to derive some glory from it. So it really hurts when that entire pretense is stripped away through calamity. Then we learn another principle of bad faith: it robs God of His glory.

True Faith Exalts in the Lord
When your faith is built on your trust in the Lord plus a confidence that your lifestyle will be considered meritorious, you actually diminish Him to the role of a butler. In contrast,
when you lay it all on the line for Him and trust Him to fulfill His promises, then you are exalting Him as the Lord of the Manor.

6. Faith and Suffering

One of the reasons for suffering is to provide Satan as a cheat and a liar.

Originally, Satan made proclamation before the entire universe that men served God only because God blesses them, and that if you remove the blessing, men would curse God to his face; that man does not see any intrinsic value in God himself, but it is only his own self-interest that makes him serve God.

But Job's suffering, in part, was sent to prove that Satan was completely wrong, i.e., that God will be served even when he does not bless any longer, because he is God, and he is worthy of the praise and the honor and service of men.

So like Job, we must learn to view the trials and tribulations that we are called on to endure as providing unique opportunities to bring glory to Him and defeat Satan, and demonstrate to those around us His power and love, so they can place their saving faith in Him also. And all of this accomplished through suffering. Thanks to Job we shall now view suffering not as a time of pain, but as a time for gain.

7. What Faith Teaches About the Character of God

When one is thrust into the fiery furnace of suffering, often, God can appear as cold, impersonal, uncaring, and demanding; a powerful Being, but lacking compassion.

But, as Job learned, behind such perceived exterior, God always acts with total compassion and completely aware of our pain, and graciously controlling everything that touches us, limiting the power of Satan and allowing certain expressions, according to his knowledge of how much we can bear.

Thanks to the Book of Job, we are able to see that in the midst of suffering, the Lord we trust, acting with patience, forgiving, and ultimately assuming responsibility for everything that happens to His children in the throes of suffering.

Conclusion

This Book reveals to us a God as a Being of incredible wisdom who puts things together far beyond the dreams and imaginations of man, who is working out incredible purposes of infinite delight and joy that he will give to us if we wait for his purposes to be worked out fully.

This book mentions a time when "the sons of God shouted with joy" {Job 38:7}, at the creation of the world, but other Scriptures tell us about a time that is coming when the sons of God will be revealed. Paul calls it "the manifestation of the sons of God" {Rom 8:19 KJV}, when all creation will shout in a greater glory than was ever hailed at creation, in the new creation, the new thing that God has brought into being by means of the sufferings, the trials, and the tribulations of this present scene.

When that day breaks, the one thing for which we will be infinitely thankful, the one thing above all others that will thrill us and cheer us and cause us to glory, is the fact that out of all the created universe we were chosen to be the ones who bore the name of God in the hour of danger and affliction, problem and trial. There is no higher honor than that.

That is what Jesus means when he says, "Blessed are you when men persecute you and say all manner of evil against you falsely for my name's sake. Rejoice and be exceeding glad, for great is your honor before the Father. For so persecuted they the prophets who were before you," {Matt 5:11-12}.

I pray that this book of Job will help us to understand the realities of life, the greatness of the privilege that has been accorded to us, and the richness of glory God heaps upon us when he allows us to suffer for his name's sake.

PART THREE:
Critical Issues of Mountain Moving Faith

In Parts One we analyzed the nature of the kind of faith that the Bible insists can move a mountain or smash a stronghold.

In Part Two we used our knowledge to study this extraordinary kind of faith as it had been modeled by certain Old Testament luminaries whose ability to practice faith-living was exemplary.

We come now to the close of our discussion about faith. We shall speak of the most critical aspects of implementing these principles into a practical lifestyle. We shall focus on three vital issues, each covered by a chapter.

Chapter 8: The Absolute Necessity of Faith
First, we shall consider the question, "Why is faith so absolutely important that you cannot live without it.

Chapter 9: Understanding Saving Faith
Next we will explore the gateway into the blessed life that God promises, especially focusing upon the gateway, which we call "saving faith". This type of faith is so powerful that it can transform a person completely opposed to the Lord into one who shares His nature, and suddenly, in this transformation, seeks to please and serve Him with the same passion that was formerly exerted in opposition to God.

Chapter 10: The Difference between Faith-Work and a Faith that Works
The faith that created the new birth into Christ now becomes the source of power to live this new life. However, it is called "faith works". The

concept creates an apparent conflict since salvation was by faith alone, and now the new life is lived by works of faith. However, the issue can be resolved in this chapter; but reconciling this apparent conflict will require the assistance of the Apostle James.

Chapter 11: Secret to Mountain Moving Faith: God's Faithfulness
Finally, we focus on the beautiful aspect of faith we have not discussed thus far—the faithfulness of God and His Word, and the influence these factors impose on genuine faith. Its an excellent note on which to end our discussion: honoring Him for one of His most important attributes.

Chapter 8

Absolute Necessity of Faith

"God does not expect us to submit our faith to him without reason, but the very limits of our reason make faith a necessity." St. Augustine.

A man fell off a cliff, but managed to grab a tree limb on the way down. The following conversation ensued: "Is anyone up there?"

"I am here. I am the Lord. Do you believe me?"

"Yes, Lord, I believe. I really believe, but I can't hang on much longer."

"That's all right; if you really believe you have nothing to worry about. I will save you. Just let go of the branch."

A moment of pause, then: "Is anyone else up there?" (*Bits & Pieces*, June 24, 1993, p. 3)

Why is it that people struggle with trusting God in their daily lives? I submit that it is because they are not yet convinced of its absolute necessity. My goal in this chapter is to offer you, dear reader, practical insights and reasons for embracing the life saving, grief sparing reality of the absolute necessity of faith in your life.

We begin with the question that, in a crisis, will loom large before you: "Why (especially when it is so hard to obey the principles of the Word in a crushing experience) cannot I resort to more pragmatic measures—i.e. why must I absolutely proceed on the basis of faith?

These are the facts that you will need to keep firmly in mind so that no matter what happens to you as a result of your personal experiences, you will understand how to react as a person of faith.

We shall approach this subject from two directions.

In the first part we shall bring to your attention insights from the Scriptures that support the contention of the absolute importance of faith. Then we shall serve you by assembling for you a list of principles that you can employ to live the life of faith in a winning manner. In this exercise, we shall attempt to act as a coach, guiding you to become a person of faith.

Part One

It is axiomatic, it is impossible to please God without faith,

Heb. 11:6 makes clear that not only must we believe that God exists, but we must believe He is a rewarder of them who diligently seek Him. This essential condition so marks the disciples of Jesus that he derives his identity from this. Hence he is called "a believer". It marks him as a person committed, first and foremost, to please God by acting in faith.

This makes sense, since his salvation resulted from his faith, likewise his new life will be marked by it. It so dominates his life that without it he cannot pray acceptably; or live victoriously; or hope to please God in anywise, because faith is the first requirement for pleasing God.

With these introductory remarks, let us examine some reasons why faith is an absolute necessity to pleasing Him in every way. We shall build our case around these principles:
- It is Commanded by God
- Its Importance is reflected in the amount of spaced the Bible gives to the subject.
- It is the true sacrifice we make on earth before Him

So, let us proceed to explain why these ideas substantiate the importance of abiding in Him.

Faith is Commanded by God

Let us return to an incident we have already discussed to glean fresh insight from it.

In the last week of his life, Jesus, while leading his disciples on a morning walk to Jerusalem from the little town of Bethany, where He had spent the night, stopped beneath a fig tree. To their amazement He cursed it. The next day, as they passed by it all could see it was obviously withered and dead. Seeing the astonishment on their faces, He said (with a note of command in His voice), "Have faith in God"). (Mark 11:14- 22)

Recall that in the first chapter we analyzed the meaning of the word "faith". To refresh your thinking, permit me to share a summary of what we discussed then. We determined that faith could be defined as "…the conviction of the truth of anything, belief; in, or a conviction or belief respecting man's relationship to God and divine things".

To amplify our understanding of the implications of this definition, let us add these ideas (convictions) to our understanding of faith:
1. The conviction that God is the creator, ruler of all things, provider and the One who bestows of all things pertaining to salvation and godly living;
2. This God is known in the Bible as Jesus is the Messiah;
3. Faith in Him results in receiving such power that one could command even a mountain to be removed and cast into the sea. Surely it was His way of saying that if their hearts were in perfect fellowship with His will, they could, by the correct exercise of faith, obtain those-things they desired.

"Have faith in God" is a plain command. Christians are commanded to exercise at this level. Surely this is borne out by the sheer amount of space the Bible devotes to the subject.

Faith is a Pre-eminent Topic of the Bible

If you want to find out what matters importantly to anyone, track his or her conversations. You will find that they usually devote more talking to this subject.

With this simple principle in mind, we investigated the amount of space devoted to the topics of "love" and "faith" in the Bible. Our findings may surprise you.

Love in the New Testament is translated, primarily, from two Greek words "phileo" and "agape". *Phileo* (brotherly love, i.e., to befriend someone) is used eighteen (18) times in the New Testament. "*Agape*" is used eighty-one (81) times (the unmerited love of God) is used eighty-one (81) times. Then we looked up all the words derived from these two inflections. That totaled 409 times. When we totaled all the times these words are mentioned, it amounted to a staggering 517 times the word "Love" appears in the Bible. So make no mistake about it, this confirms how important love is, especially the love God extends to us, as Believers, and expresses through us to those He loves.

Then I looked up this word "faith". I was a bit astonished. The Greek word, "*Pistis*", and its derivations, "belief" and "trust" occur a total of 868 times.

Next, I tried to get an idea of how prevalent is the mention of one of these words associated with "faith". To do this, I divided the number of chapters that comprise the Bible (1,169), by the number of times this word is mentioned (868). As I did the math, I realized that the word "faith" is mentioned about every one and a quarter chapter. It is difficult to preach the Bible without preaching faith, because it is everywhere in the Book. In fact, the word *faith* is mentioned about 351 times more than *love* in the Bible. That experiment proves just how pre-eminent faith is to the mind and will of God, else, why would He have devoted so much text to the subject?

In Paul's classic statement about the subjects of faith and love, he wrote (in I Corinthians 13), "Now abideth faith, hope and charity, the greatest of these is charity (or love). The implication is that while love is greatest; still, faith is first, i.e., that one cannot have love without faith, or hope to receive anything from God without faith. Everything you receive is by faith… "not by works of righteousness which we have done but according to His mercy He said to us" and faith is not of ourselves. It is the gift of God."

Faith as a Type of Sacrificial Offering

Let us return to a verse we have previously examined:

> Heb. 11:6. *And without faith it is impossible to please Him. They that come to Him must believe that He is, and that He is a rewarder of them that diligently seek Him."*

Faith is so vital that without it, we cannot please God. Later in this chapter the writer adds, that we must not only believe that God exists, but we must believe that He is a "rewarder of those that "diligently seek" Him".

As we analyze two key words ("rewarder" and "diligently seek") we discover that the first word means "one who is a payer, or giver of wages". The second one means to "thoroughly seek out". To understand the point we are making, think of the diligence with which a parent would expend in looking for a missing child at a seaside park in a crowd.

Please do not miss the implications of these words in combination: they convey the idea that the person who seeks the Lord and trusts Him unreservedly will have the tangible things added to his life.

Of course this idea must be considered in the context of other Biblical principles, e.g., the one about "Seek ye first the kingdom of God and all these things will be added unto you". But the implication remains, He is a giver of good things including wages to those who seek His fellowship and His will with a diligence based on love (*agape*) for Him.

It also has implications regarding *phileo* love. Faith enables us to extend mercy to those who offend us. Faith is a necessary ingredient for forgiveness; it figures in two important areas:

- It is crucial to receiving blessings from the Lord, since if we do not forgive, we will not be forgiven; and without this condition met, we cannot ask or receive anything from God.
- It is also crucial in receiving forgiveness; since it is involved in receiving forgiveness after we repent. Without this faith factor, people cannot receive God's forgiveness. (You cannot imagine the people I have counseled who were miserable because they could not, by faith, simply receive God's forgiveness). To do otherwise leaves us living in guilt and condemnation, not realizing that we are truly forgiven.

Faith That Moves Mountains and Smashes Strongholds

So this type of relational love impacts our faith. To help you appreciate this truth, permit me to share with you this story.

One night a house caught fire and a young boy was forced to flee to the roof. The father stood on the ground below with outstretched arms, calling to his son, "Jump! I'll catch you." He knew the boy had to jump to save his life. All the boy could see, however, was flame, smoke, and blackness. As can be imagined, he was afraid to leave the roof. His father kept yelling: "Jump! I will catch you." But the boy protested, "Daddy, I can't see you." The father replied, "But I can see you and you know of my love (as your father), and that's all that matters."

Genuine Faith: Quality Matters

Declaring that God is able to do that which we trust Him for, and, then approaching Him without any lingering doubt produce the quality of faith that can move any mountain. Notice that these requirements ignore any mention of *quantity* of faith (usually measured by the amount of passion or confidence one feels).

Trust me; the kind of faith that brings "mountain moving" results depends totally upon its quality, not its quantity. A story involving Hudson Taylor illustrates my point.

During an especially trying time in the work of the China Inland Mission, Hudson Taylor wrote to his wife, "We have twenty-five cents-- and all the promises of God! Faith totally trusting in those promises plus any amount is sufficient for God's supply.

Once, Taylor, while enroute demonstrated the purity of his faith while making a voyage on a sailing vessel. As it neared the channel between the southern Malay Peninsula and the island of Sumatra, the missionary heard an urgent knock on his stateroom door.

He opened it, and there stood the captain of the ship. "Mr. Taylor," he said, "we have no wind. We are drifting toward an island where the people are heathen, and I fear they are cannibals." "What can I do?" asked Taylor. "I understand that you believe in God. I want you to pray for wind."

"All right, Captain, I will, but you must set the sail."

"Why that's ridiculous! There's not even the slightest breeze. Besides, the sailors will think I'm crazy." But finally, because of Taylor's insistence, he agreed.

Forty-five minutes later he returned and found the missionary still on his knees. "You can stop praying now," said the captain. "We've got more wind than we know what to do with!"

Taylor was such a man of faith because he saw that true faith was as essential to answered prayer as wind to the movement of that sail boat. Likewise, with us, our pure faith will move the throne of God to answer our prayers.

Genuine Faith Dispels Doubt as It Grows Stronger

Paul wrote to the Thessalonians, "*We are bound to give thank…because that your faith grows exceedingly…*" (2 Thess. 1:3). Another benefit of living by faith is that with each succeeding experience of triumph, your ability to trust Him for greater things actually increases, and the less likely we fall into a doubting mode.

By way of illustrations, we have observed, Hudson Taylor, a man who demonstrated that he approached the throne of Grace seeking the supply of his needs with great boldness. But such faith started somewhere. It began before he ever left England for China. What we have described grew from such experiences as the following one while a student in preparation. Permit me to illustrate from his life again.

As a young man preparing to go to China, Hudson Taylor determined to learn to live by faith alone while he was still in England. His resolve was "to learn before leaving England to move man through God by prayer alone." He worked for a doctor and was paid quarterly. When the time drew near to receive his salary, Taylor was disturbed that his employer said nothing about it. Taylor had only one half-crown piece, but he determined not to break his resolution and ask for his salary.

While visiting a needy home on the Lord's Day, Taylor felt led of God to give his last coin to the needy family. The next day he received an anonymous gift through the mail, four times what he had given to the poor! The following Saturday, the doctor finished up his work and said, "Taylor, is not your salary due again?" Taylor told him that it was and became disappointed when he learned that the doctor had forgotten about the salary due and sent all his funds to the bank! He prayed about the matter (for he had bills of his own to pay) and left it with the Lord. That evening, the doctor visited him and said that one of his richest patients had come over after hours to pay his bill! He gave the money to Taylor, who rejoiced. He had learned he could trust God and therefore go to China as a missionary.

As one observes the path of progress of this missionary statesman, one realizes that he is a living example of the principle: the more we feed our faith, the surer our doubts will starve to death. The more we feed on the Word of God the greater will be our spiritual growth. The Holy Spirit will both fertilize and stimulate this growth process so that we can be "nourished up in the word of faith". The Word becomes like a perfect soil in which faith can grow.

George Mueller sums up the point we are making when he wrote, "God delights to increase the faith of His children...I say, and say it deliberately--trials, difficulties and sometimes defeat, are the very food of faith...We should take them out of His hands as evidences of His love and care for us in developing more and more that faith which He is seeking to strengthen in us".

Genuine Faith Is a Protector

Paul concludes the Book of Ephesians by describing the armor that the Believer needs to put on to deal with spiritual battles. Notice that a strategic piece of protection is the "above all, put on the shield of faith" (Eph. 6:16).

From this truth two facts emerge:
- The Christian life is one of incessant spiritual warfare, a daily occurrence in the believer's walk and life; and,
- This shield is of the utmost importance.

Faith is so effective in protecting us from spiritual attack that Paul could say elsewhere, that by use of faith as a protective tactic, nothing can ultimately harm us, therefore, "*in all these things we are more than conquerors through Him who loved us*", (Rom. 8:37).

Absolute Necessity of Faith

Permit me to tell you about Susannah, a little girl who used faith as a shield to protect the life of her little brother from the ravages of brain cancer.

She learned of her brother's critical illness by overhearing her parents discussing the doctor's diagnosis. She learned that the only way to save his life was by surgery. So she knelt by her bed and asked God to provide the operation.

For two weeks she worked and saved and accumulated $13.49 in her piggy bank. This was the amount she had, so she set out to find the surgeon for her brother, confident that the funds at hand were sufficient.

She visited the only place she knew, a local pharmacy. There she attempted to get the attention of the druggist, but he was talking with another adult and kept ignoring her. Finally, he could not do so and turned to her with some impatience and said, "Little girl, can't you see that I am talking with this gentleman. Please do not interrupt until I finish.

But, she did interrupt: "Sir, I am sorry, but I have to find a surgeon for my brother. I have money to pay for it.

The man talking with the pharmacist turned to her and said, "Tell me, young lady, what is the nature of your brother's problem?

"He has a cancer tumor, sir" she blurted out., and he will die if he does not get an operation. I have been saving up to pay for it.

The man then asked her, "How much money do you have for such an operation?

She replied that she had $13.49. Suddenly he saw the passion of her faith, her solid assurance, and he began to smile.

"Well, my young friend, you are in great luck. It just so happens that I know a surgeon who will perform that operation for exactly that amount of money".

Of course she had encountered a world famous brain surgeon who performed the surgery for the prescribed amount. Was it chance? Was it coincidence? No it was the work of faith that was looking to the Lord as a shield to guard the life of her brother.

Faith is the best shield, isn't it?

Part Two: A Coach's List of Strategic Benefits of Faith

We Trinidadians occasionally get the opportunity to observe an American style football game on television. I asked an American friend why the coaches carry those small cards in their hands that they keep referring to. He said that those cards have several important plays, which are so intricate that the coach has to have a written reference to help him call them in to the players (who have their positions already memorized). Upon hearing this, I thought, "And I thought our game of Cricket was complex (which it is)?

To live the life of faith effectively before the Lord Jesus, you will need to always understand certain essential facts. Think of them as the knowledge so important to the ongoing game of life that they are worth writing on a card and carrying in your pocket.

Surely, as we pursue the game of life, as a person of faith, we can benefit from having, at hand, solid Biblical promises from which we can use, without having to recall them from memory.

To this end, I thought it would be helpful to prepare for you a list of many specific and essential ways in which the Bible speaks. Of course if we analyzed them all completely, this book would be too large. So, we will only list these areas of our Christian life where faith plays an absolutely vital role, and figures so importantly:

1. We cannot be saved without faith (John 3:36).
2. We cannot live victoriously over the world without faith (1 John 5:4).
3. We cannot please God without faith (Heb. 11:6).
4. We cannot pray without faith (James 1:6).
5. We cannot have peace with God without faith (Romans 5:1).
6. We cannot have joy without faith (1 Pet. 1:7).
7. We are justified by faith and not by works (Gal. 2:16).
8. We are to live by faith (Gal. 2:20).
9. We are made righteous by faith (Rom. 10:1-4).
10. Christ dwells in our heart by faith (Eph. 3;17).
11. The Holy Spirit is received by faith (Gal. 3:2).
12. "Whatever is not of faith is sin" (Rom. 14:23).
13. Faith and doubt don't mix. (Matthew 21:21)
14. Others will recognize the exercise of true faith. (Rom. 1:8; Col. 1:4)

15. God has given the measure of faith to everyone. (Romans 12:3).
16. Follow the examples of people of faith (Hebrews 6:12)
17. The trying of your faith works patience (James 1:3)
18. The prayer of faith will heal the sick (James 5:15)
19. The trial of your faith would be found as a praise to the Lord (1 Peter 1:7)

In summary, faith is important because it honors God, and God always honors faith.

To exhaust the importance of faith would require several volumes, which would contain myriads of Biblical examples and explanations, which are not presently possible for this book. However, we have given enough examples to provide you with adequate explanations in an effort to excite you to pursue the life of faith.

Remember, since Faith is so very important in the eyes of God, it should be considered as the utmost importance to us. After all, we are called believers. Everything hinges on faith, as the experience of this young photographer illustrates.

In April 1988 the evening news reported on a photographer who was a skydiver. He had jumped from a plane along with numerous other skydivers and filmed the group as they fell and opened their parachutes. On the film shown on the telecast, as the final skydiver opened his chute, the picture went berserk.

The announcer reported that the cameraman had fallen to his death, having jumped out of the plane without his parachute. It wasn't until he reached for the absent ripcord that he realized he was freefalling without a parachute. Until that point, the jump probably seemed exciting and fun. But tragically, he had acted with thoughtless haste and deadly foolishness. Nothing could save him, for his faith was in a parachute that he had never buckled on.

Faith in anything but an all-sufficient God can be just as tragic spiritually. Only with faith in Jesus Christ dare we step into the dangerous excitement of life.

Martin Luther summed up the point of this chapter when he wrote, "God our Father has made all things depend on faith so that whoever has faith will have everything, and whoever does not have faith will have nothing."

Chapter 9

Understanding Saving Faith

"The N.T. never says that a man is saved on account of his faith, but always that he is saved through his faith, or by means of his faith; faith is merely the means which the Holy Spirit uses to apply to the individual soul the benefits of Christ's death." J. Gresham Machen, What Is Faith, p. 180

The African impala can jump to a height of over 10 feet and cover a distance of greater than 30 feet. Yet these magnificent creatures can be kept in an enclosure in any zoo with a 3-foot wall. The animals will not jump if they cannot see where their feet will fall.

Faith is the ability to trust what we cannot see, and with faith we are freed from the flimsy enclosures of life that only fear allows to entrap us. Certainly there is no situation in life where one is required to exercise faith with no regard for the landing spot, than in saving faith.

Saving Faith and Works

In this chapter we shall present the case of faith for justification; while in the next chapter we shall demonstrate the faith of sanctification. While, in regard to saving faith, we will make the case for it being strictly a work of grace to produce faith without works, still, in salvation there is a type of works that we should mention at the outset.

To explain the balance between work and faith in saving faith, permit me to share the comments of Martin Luther on this subject:

> "The question is asked: how can justification take place without the works of the law, even though James says: 'Faith without works is dead'? In answer, the apostle distinguishes between the law and faith, the letter and grace. The 'works of the law' are works done without faith and grace, by the law, which forces them to be done through fear or the enticing promise of temporal advantages. But 'works of faith' are those done in the spirit of liberty, purely out of love to God. And only those who are justified by faith can do them. An ape can cleverly imitate the actions of humans. But he is not therefore a human. If he became a human, it would undoubtedly be not by virtue of the works by which he imitated man but by virtue of something else; namely, by an act of God. Then, having been made a human, he would perform the works of humans in proper fashion. Paul does not say that faith is without its characteristic works, but that it justifies without the works of the law. Therefore justification does not require the works of the law; but it does require a living faith, which performs its works."

Now, we are ready to make the case for saving faith; the kind that results in the glorious reality of salvation.

Why Saving Faith Matters

Christianity is a faith that is intended to be experienced as a lifestyle. As a result, it is a fragile thing, easily marginalized and weakened by small sin actions that prevent the Holy Spirit from guiding the human spirit. As a result, this individual begins to live like an unbeliever, without supernatural resources. The problem then is that this person still feels the need to try to please God—but no power to do so!

The Apostle Paul spoke to this problem. He said that walking in the Spirit involves continually making decisions that seem like small issues but carry large consequences. To provide his point, he used two analogies. He likened these actions to operating a ship's rudder. This small tool can determine a ship's direction. Paul also illustrated the same point using a "bit" in a horse's mouth. It also is very small, but can control a very large animal in full gallop.

What is the single issue of each decision? It is this: to act in faith, or act independently of the will of God. The central role that faith plays in the life of a true believer actually begins with the very process of salvation. In this experience, failure to properly exercise faith results in a religious proselyte instead of a regenerated person. So, analyzing this experience, and faith's role, can help you appreciate how important it is in every moment that you draw breath as a saved person.

The Role of Faith in Salvation

The second chapter of Ephesians offers a most instructive step-by step analysis of the process by which one comes from a state of being "…dead in trespasses and in sin." (Eph.2:1) to the state of being "…saved by grace through faith" (Eph. 2:8)

A careful exegesis will make clear that the process follows a very precise path of progression.

1. The Spirit of God, using the Word of God, (Romans 10) touches the human heart with a sense of "lost-ness". This sense is based on three truths that the Holy Spirit reveals to your spirit:
- God can be your Father
- Jesus can be your Lord
- Your sins can be forgiven

We know this because each of these phrases is introduced by the phrase, "we know…" and the word means, "to be shown", much like in a vision. It is truth that suddenly the mind becomes aware of, that otherwise, would not be known.

2. What is the purpose of this convicting work of the Spirit? To bring about *repentance*!

Repentance is the first thing that a person can do to bring about true salvation. That repentance will be discussed later in this chapter. For now, consider this question: What is the purpose of true repentance?

Understanding Saving Faith

The purpose of true repentance is to satisfy the demand of God to come to Him with nothing of human merit, and seeking Him as a man would seek a piece of timber to support him when stranded in the ocean after a shipwreck.

As a result of this confession of sin and true repentance, the Lord gives this broken soul a new ability that he never possessed before. True, all people have the ability to exercise faith, but only the Spirit of God can give you the gift of faith that can be exercised in such a way as to move His heart to give you a supernatural gift.

3. The Gift of Faith.
True repentance results in the gift of faith. Praise God, for this is the only kind of faith that God will accept for the salvation Ephesians 2:8 describes: "…through faith are you saved…" Without this, one is attempting to gain eternal life by giving to God human faith—and this will produce a sincere proselyte but not a soul capable of living forever.

Thank God for this "unspeakable gift". This gift makes it possible to achieve the impossible—to be genuinely saved. That final step will involve you doing the second thing: using this faith to trust the Lord Jesus as your personal Savior.

4. Trusting in Jesus as Lord and Savior
The person under conviction takes the faith he has been given by the Holy Spirit and with it, places his full faith and confidence in trusting the Lord Jesus to become his personal Savior and Lord. With this sincere step of faith certain things occur.

- The Spirit presents your heartfelt placement of your faith in Jesus.
- The Son then petitions the Father to grant you salvation and make you His Son (so you can now call the Father Abba).
- The Father, observing that the sacrifice of the Son truly covers all sin—including that of the penitent heart, and grants you the privilege of being His Son. As a result two things happen next:
- First, the Son authorizes the Holy Spirit, as His proxy, to dwell in your newly created human spirit so that the one who indwells is legally Christ, but in actuality, is the Holy Spirit.

- The Holy Spirit performs a miracle within your spirit to create a new spirit where God can commune with you and then He takes up residence within that new spirit to begin to fulfill the purpose of God for your life through you.

5. Receiving, by Grace, Full Salvation.

Suddenly the things that were originally used to confront this person with the three most important things in life he lacks (mentioned above), and convict him of his alienation from God and his being under eternal damnation, are realities this individual not only possesses but knows that he does.

6. Presence of Joy

The Bible says that the believer, to confirm the reality of his salvation, will experience a heart response that is not possible apart from the work of the Holy Spirit. Anyone can experience happiness; but only a true believer, under the influence of the Holy Spirit can experience the joy of the His response is a genuine mark of authenticity; he experiences the joy of the Lord.

Small wonder that Paul calls this supernatural transaction a GIFT and describes it with this simple phrase: "By grace are you save, through (the gift of) faith…" (Eph. 2:8).

He then says, "As you have received (faith) (for your salvation), so walk in faith". Paul's point: the same principle by which our life in Christ began—the exercise of the gift of "faith" is also the same way by which we continue to live in Him until He calls us to glory. (This topic of how to use faith to live the Christian life will be discussed in the next chapter).

Now we are focusing on the nature of the saving faith, since it plays such an eternally significant role in bringing you from darkness unto a state of righteousness ready for heaven.

Since faith plays such a critical role in salvation, Satan seeks to trick you with counterfeit faith; and he has devised clever, pious sounding religious "knock-off" belief systems. How can we protect people from being taken in by false religious "faiths"? We shall provide you some counsel so that by understanding these "knock-offs" you will also gain a healthy understanding of what real faith entails.

What Saving Faith "Aint"

"There is a generation that is pure in their own eyes, and yet is not washed from their filthiness" (Proverbs 30:12). This verse describes people who rely on baptism, church-membership or their own moral and religious performances as their hope for salvation.

These people are also described by this verse, "There is a way that seems right unto a man, but the end thereof are the ways of death" (Proverbs 14:12).

It is easy to assume that this problem centers only on false Gospels; but it also involves the wrong use of the true Gospel.

Within the evangelical church there are many who embrace the right doctrine. They are convinced that Christ alone can save any sinner, this has become a settled creed, from which neither man or the Devil can shake them. So far so good.

But the trap lies in the way in which they respond to this truth. In an effort to show great responses, preachers invite them to respond with a gesture that does not require true repentance, therefore, does not produce saving faith. The result is a sincere church member, but not a regenerated believer. This problem is called, "easy believism". It is the result of a terrible malady that has gripped church development. Leaders see the need for building large congregations. They resort to a strategy of ministry popularized as "marketing model". This attempt to gain converts without confronting people of the reality of sin and hell, invites them to make such simple, innocuous gesture of faith. For many of these people, salvation never happens.

It is easy to see that in a cultic church, or a church led by a modernist pulpiteer would fail to present the true Gospel. But the subtlety of Satan is that he can work his tragic magic in churches with a strong Biblical doctrine.

Why does this failure occur? Because these churches, catering to the post-modern pew, become fearful of offending people who do not like to hear such truths as "hell" and "damnation" and "eternal fiery judgment". I confess that I would like to preach a warm "fuzzy" Gospel message that made it easy for sinners to sin under my ministry without ever becoming uncomfortable. But I choose to serve the Lord and a sinner's true heart needs; and thus forego the opportunity to become a "good guy".

Faith That Moves Mountains and Smashes Strongholds

Jesus had to deal with this same problem (believing in Christ that does not result in salvation). In John 8:30 we are told, "As He spoke these words, many believed on Him," mark carefully it is not merely said "many believed in Him," but "many believed on Him." Nevertheless, one does not have to read much farther on in the chapter to discover that those very people were unregenerate and unsaved souls.

In John 5:44 we find the Lord telling similar "believers" that they were of their father the Devil; and in John 5:59 we find them taking up stones to cast at Him.

This has presented a real difficulty unto some; yet it ought not. They created their own difficulty, by supposing that faith in Christ necessarily saves. It does not. *There is a faith in Christ which saves, and there is also a faith in Christ which does not save.*

To illustrate, let us learn from this verse: "Among the chief rulers also many believed on him." Were, then, those men saved?

Many preachers and evangelists, as well as tens of thousands of their blinded dupes, would answer, "Most assuredly!" But let us note what immediately follows here: "But because of the Pharisees they did not confess him, lest they should be put out of the synagogue: for they loved the praise of men more than the praise of God" (John 12:42, 43).

Will any of our readers now say that those men were saved? If so, it is clear proof that you are utter strangers to any saving work of God in your own souls.

Men who are afraid to hazard the loss of their worldly positions, temporal interests, personal reputations, or any thing else that is dear to them, for Christ's sake, are yet in their sins—no matter how they may be trusting in Christ's finished work to take them to Heaven.

Probably most of our readers have been brought up under the teaching that there are only two classes of people in this world, Believers and Unbelievers. But such a classification is misleading, and erroneous. God's Word, in the following verse, "give none offense (I Cor. 10:32) goes on to distinguish three classes of people we re not to offend: 1) Jews, nor 2) Gentiles, nor 3) the church of God".

Notice that the first class is the "Gentile" or Heathen nations, outside the commonwealth of Israel, which formed by far the largest class. Corresponding with that class today are the countless millions of modern heathen, who are "lovers of pleasure more than lovers of God."

Second, there was the Nation of Israel, which has to be subdivided into two groups, for as Romans 9:6 declares, "They are not all Israel which are of Israel." By far, the larger portion of the nation of Israel was made up of people who were only the nominally, i.e., outwardly believers in the Messiah. I see these as similar to the great mass of empty professors bearing the name of Christ today.

Third, there was the spiritual remnant of Israel, whose calling, hope, and inheritance was heavenly: corresponding to them in this day are the genuine Christians, God's "little flock" (Luke 12:32).

The same threefold division among men is plainly discernible throughout John's Gospel.

First, there were the hardened leaders of the Nation, the scribes and Pharisees, priests and elders. From start to finish they were openly opposed to Christ, and neither His blessed teaching nor wondrous works had any melting effects upon them.

Second, there was the common people who "heard Him gladly" (Mark 12:37), a great many of whom are said to have "believed on Him" (see John 2:23; 7:31; 8:30; 10:42; 11:45; 12:11), but concerning whom there is nothing to show that they were saved. They were not outwardly opposed to Christ, but they never yielded their hearts to Him. They were impressed by His Divine credentials, yet were easily offended (John 6:66).

Third, there was the insignificant handful who "received Him" (John 1:12) into their hearts and lives; received Him as their Lord and Savior.

The same three classes are clearly discernible (to anointed eyes) in the world today.

First, there are the vast multitudes who make no profession at all, who see nothing in Christ that they should desire Him; people who are deaf to every appeal, and who make little attempt to conceal their hatred of the Lord Jesus.

Second, there is that large company who are attracted by Christ in a natural way. So far from being openly antagonistic to Him and His cause, they are found among His followers. Having been taught much of the Truth, they "believe in Christ," just as children reared by conscientious Mohammedans believe firmly and devoutly in Mohammed. Having received much instruction concerning the virtues of Christ's precious blood, they trust in its merits to deliver them from the wrath to come; and yet there is nothing in their daily lives to show that they are new creatures in Christ Jesus!

Third, there are the "few" (Matthew 7:13, 14) who deny themselves, take up the cross daily, and follow a despised and rejected Christ in the path of loving and unreserved obedience unto God.

From this analysis of the categories of belief, you can see that there is a faith in Christ, which saves; but there is a faith in Christ, which does not save.

I recognize that this discussion reflects a hard truth. But I urge you, dear reader, not to give in to the urge to weaken it by saying that faith in Christ, which does not save, is merely an historical faith, or, where there is a believing about Christ instead of believing in Him. Not so. By "historical faith" we mean "head knowledge about Him that falls short of being a quickening and saving faith.

What, then, does saving faith consist of? In seeking to answer this question our present object is not only to supply a Scriptural definition, but one, which at the same time, differentiates it from a non-saving faith. This is no easy task, for the two, often have much in common: that faith in Christ which does not save, has in it more than one element or ingredient of that which does vitally unite the soul to Him.

The tightrope that must be walked:
- Not to elevate the standard higher than the Bible does, and thereby discourage true believers by humanly imposed "work" related requirements; and,
- Not to lower the standard below that which the Bible requires for repentance, and commitment, thereby producing unregenerate professors.

In drawing careful lines about the true nature of saving faith, it is not our wish to withhold from the people of God their legitimate portion; or to commit the sin of taking the children's bread and casting it to the dogs. May the Holy Spirit Himself carefully guide you, dear reader, to understand the point we are attempting to make.

A Biblical Definition of Unbelief

To arrive at a clear understanding of saving faith, it is helpful first to get a clear idea of the character of unbelief. Permit me to sketch the religious type faith that does not lead to salvation (i.e., is not saving faith).

- Hearty assent unto what God's Word sets forth
- An error in judgment
- Failure to believe deeply enough, the truth
- It is a clever, virulent, violent opposition to God.

Unbelief has a passive and active, as well as a negative and a positive side. All of this appears in the translations of the Greek noun and verb:

Noun:
- "Unbelief" (negative, passive) (Romans 11:20; Hebrews 4:6, 11)
- "Disobedience" (positive, active) (Ephesians 2:2; 5:6).

Verb
- "Believed not" (active, negative) (Hebrews 3:18; 11:31) and
- "Obey not" (active, negative) (1 Peter 3:1; 4:17).

Perhaps a few concrete examples will help us make this point clearer.

Example: Adam

Assumption: He failed to believe God's solemn threat that in the day He should eat of the forbidden fruit he would surely die.

Truth: "by one man's disobedience many were made sinners" (Romans 5:19).

Therefore, his actions were not passive; he willfully committed the act of disobedience that produced the Fall.

Assumption: The heinousness of our first parent's sin consisted in listening to the lie of the Serpent.

Truth:
- 1 Timothy 2:14 expressly declare, "Adam was not deceived."
- He was determined to have his own way, no matter what God had prohibited and threatened.

Thus, the very first case of unbelief in human history consisted not only in negatively failing to take to heart what God had so clearly and so solemnly said, but also in deliberate defying and rebelling against Him.

Example: Israel in Wilderness

Fact: "They could not enter in (the Promised Land) because of unbelief" (Hebrews 3:19).

Assumption: Those words mean that they missed Canaan because of their failure to appropriate the promise of God?

Truth: The promise of entering Canaan was given to them. They failed to receive it in faith (Heb. 4:1, 2). God had declared that the seed of Abraham should inherit that land flowing with milk and honey. As a result, it was the privilege of that generation which was delivered from Egypt to lay hold of and apply that promise to them.

Assumption: they lost out on entering Canaan because they failed to receive it in faith (Hebrews 4:1, 2).

Truth: They lost out because they not only failed to receive it by faith, but also because of the two following factors:
- Their unbelief caused them to openly disobey God. When the spies brought back a sample of the goodly grapes, and Joshua urged them to go up and possess the land, they refused. Accordingly Moses declared, "Notwithstanding ye would not go up, but rebelled against the commandment of the Lord your God" (Deut.1:26).
- Their unbelief caused them to become self-willed, disobedient, and defiant.

Example: People Who Heard Jesus

Observe the reaction to those contemporaries of His earthly ministry who heard Him teaching the Word. Notice their reaction as John 1:11, and 12 described it:
- "He came unto his own, and his own received him not" In the next verse, this "receiving not" is defined as "they believed" Him not".

Assumption: They were guilty of nothing more than a failure to assent to Jesus' teaching and trust in His person.

Truth: They were guilty of this and also of hating Him (John 15:25), and therefore, refusing "to come to Him" (John 5:40). Later they explain why. His holy demands did not suit their fleshly desires; therefore they said, "We will not have this man to reign over us" (Luke 19:14). Thus, their unbelief too, consisted in the spirit of self-will and open defiance, a determination to please themselves at all costs.

Unbelief is not simply an infirmity of fallen human nature. It is a heinous crime. Scripture everywhere attributes it to love of sin, obstinacy of will, and hardness of heart.

Unbelief has its root in a depraved nature, in a mind, which is enmity against God. Love of sin is the immediate cause of unbelief: "And this is the condemnation, that light is come into the world, and men loved darkness rather than light, because their deeds were evil" (John 3:19).

When a person hears the Gospel, and discovers that it aims to separate him from his sins, many suddenly want no more to do with it, especially when the following facts are made clear from the pulpit:
1. Saving faith then is the opposite of damning unbelief.
2. Both issue from the heart:
   - Unbelief, from a heart that is alienated from God, which is in a state of rebellion against Him;
   - Saving faith, from a heart, which is reconciled to Him and so has ceased to fight against Him.

Perhaps, if the Gospel were more clearly and faithfully preached, fewer would profess to believe it; but the people who did embrace the Gospel and find Christ as their Savior would be stronger and more stable in their walk and worship.

What Is Saving Faith

Now, permit me to describe the essential elements that characterize saving faith:
- It is a yielding to the authority of God, a submitting of one's self to His rule.
- It is much more than understanding essential facts, assenting to the fact that Christ is a Savior for sinners, and that He stands ready to receive all who trust in Him.
- To be received by Christ, I must come to Him renouncing all my own righteousness (Rom.10:3), as an empty-handed beggar (Matt. 19:21), but I must also forsake my self-will and rebellion against Him (Psa. 2:11,12; Prov. 28:13).
- Saving faith is a genuine coming to Christ: Matthew 28; John 6:37, etc.

- The clear and inevitable implication of this phrase, "coming" to Christ: something has to be left out—the negative aspect. Think about it: If I am going to Tobago, I obviously have had to leave some place. Likewise to come to Christ automatically implies that something has to have been left—i.e. the old lifestyle, the "way of sinners" (Psalm 1). But if this term is not made clear then the person hearing it might easily misunderstand what must be abandoned in order to properly place one's true hope and faith in the Lord. So what is this that must be left behind?

This raises the question, what is it that I must leave behind:

i) Every false object of confidence, or hope
ii) All other competitors for my heart. "For ye were 'as sheep going astray;' but are now returned unto the Shepherd and Bishop of your souls" (1 Peter 2:25). And what is meant by "ye were (note the past tense; it means that they were doing this, but are no longer so doing) as sheep going astray"? Isaiah 53:6 tells us: "All we like sheep have gone astray; we have turned every one to his own way." That is what must be forsaken before we can truly "come" to Christ.
iii) The course of self-will must be abandoned. The prodigal son could not come to his father while he remained in the far country.

Dear reader, if you are still following a course of self-pleasing, you are only deceiving yourself if you think you have come to Christ.

John Bunyan summed this up, "Coming to Christ is attended with an honest and sincere forsaking all for Him—(here he quotes Luke 14:26,27). By these and like expressions elsewhere, Christ describes the true comer: he is one that casts all behind his back."

There are a great many "pretended comers" to Jesus Christ in the world. They remind me of the man Jesus spoke about in a parable: (Matt. 21:30) who committed to serving his father by telling him, 'I go sir", but, in reality, he never kept his word ("…but went not.").

These people respond to the Gospel with a verbal commitment, but in reality, cannot dislodge themselves from their pleasures and carnal delights. They either do not understand that to place one's faith in Christ involves repentance, self-abnegation as well as leaving of all false confidences, as well as renouncing all love to sin. It means to look to Jesus as the only solitary pillar of our confidence and hope.

Saving faith consists of the complete surrender of my whole being and life to the claims of God upon me. It is the unreserved acceptance of Christ, not only as my Savior, but as my absolute Lord, bowing to His will and receiving His yoke. In fact, wherever the terms are found together the order is always, "Lord and Savior," and never vice versa: see Luke 1:46, 47; 2 Peter 1:11; 2:20; 3:18.

When Saving Faith is Evident

Until I, as an ungodly person, became, through the Spirit's leading, aware of the exceeding sinfulness of my self-pleasing life, and became genuinely broken and repentant before God, and willingly forsook the world for Christ and placed myself under His controlling Lordship, my turning the Christ as my Savior and Lord would have not been sufficient to move God to grant me salvation.

Recognizing this, you can imagine my shock at much that passes for evangelistic preaching today that makes no such demands upon the soul of the lost.

As previously mentioned, I call this his substitute Gospel "Easy Believe-ism". It produces no genuine salvation because it invites a sinner to come to Christ without making true repentance, and without a clear understanding of that it requires a real love for him that demonstrates its genuineness by obedience to Him and His Word

So what are the proofs of saving faith?

Reformation is not regeneration, and a changed life does not always indicate a changed heart. The question becomes very important when you realize that the heart of the unsaved person is thoroughly depraved. Its thoughts, imaginations, desires and affections are corrupt. Hence, the first real work of faith is to cleanse the soul from these pollutions. The human heart is so fickle that it is difficult to actually know the true intent of one's mind.

Imagine that you were attempting to help a person infected with the dreaded HIV condition. You heard that a vaccine was available and you obtained a dose for this person.

He begins his treatment. But shortly, he begins to ignore the clear directions prescribed for using the medication in treatment, and violates the rules for taking care of his own health along with the medication. As a result, a mutant variety of the HIV disease begins to grow in his body, for which there was no vaccine, and for which the current vaccine was completely ineffective. What would you say to that person?

Now imagine that you have a friend who is infected with a sin nature, and will, if nothing is done, spend eternity in Hell. So you reach out to share with them the true Gospel, and urge them to place their faith correctly in the Lord Jesus. They say many fine sounding things, and yet, shortly, you discover that they have returned to the lifestyle that characterized those without Christ. Would you conclude that the faith they expressed was inadequate? You would be correct—it is not saving faith; because when God imparts saving faith to a soul, radical and real effects will follow.

One cannot be raised from the dead without there being a consequent walking in newness of life. One cannot be the subject of a miracle of grace being wrought in the heart without a noticeable change being apparent to all who know him. Where a supernatural root has been implanted, supernatural fruit must issue from it. There will now be in evidence a yearning after perfection, a spirit resisting the flesh, a striving against sin, a growing in grace, and a pressing forward along the "narrow way" which leads to Heaven.

As Titus 3:5 so plainly affirms, God "saved us by the washing of regeneration, and renewing of the Holy Spirit"; and it is the presence of His "fruit" in my heart and life, which furnishes the immediate evidence of my salvation.

"With the heart man believeth unto righteousness" (Romans 10:10).

God's Word speaks of "purifying their hearts by faith" (Acts 15:9). What is meant by this phrase? It has to do with cleansing the following areas of the heart-condition:
1. Purifying of the understanding, by the illumination of the Word to cleanse the mind from error.
2. Purifying the conscience, so as to cleanse it from guilt.
3. Purifying of the will, so as to cleanse it from self-will and self-seeking.

4. Purifying of the affections, so as to cleanse them from the love of all that is evil.

In Scripture the "heart" includes all these four faculties. A deliberate purpose to continue in any one sin cannot consist with a pure heart.

So what are the results of this purification? What will be the marks of such a heart? They will include the following characteristics.

First the heart purified by regeneration will become **Humble**.

Faith lays the soul low, for it discovers its own vileness, emptiness, and impotency. Faith empties a man of self-conceit, self-confidence, and self-righteousness, and makes him seem nothing, in order that Christ may become all in all. The strongest faith will always be accompanied by the greatest humility. (Matt. 8:8- 10).

Second, the regenerated heart will become **Tender**:

"A new heart also will I give you, and a new spirit will I put within you: and I will take away the stony heart out of your flesh, and I will give you a heart of flesh" (Ezekiel 36:26). An unregenerate heart is as hard as a stone, full of pride and presumption. But a regenerated heart is moved by the love of Christ, and says, "How can I sin against His incredibly selfless love for me?" When overtaken by a fault, a regenerate heart experiences a passionate relenting and bitter mourning over his sin.

Third, the purified Hear **Works by love**

It is not inactive, but energetic. It diffuses spiritual energy to all the faculties of the soul, then enlists them in the service of God. Faith is a principle of life by which the Christian lives unto God; a principle of motion, by which he walks to Heaven, along the highway of holiness; a principle of strength, by which he opposes the flesh, the world, and the Devil.

A newborn infant cannot walk and work as a grown man. Yet it breathes and cries, moves and sucks, and thereby shows it is alive. So with the one who has been born again: there is a breathing unto God, a crying after Him, a moving toward Him, a clinging to Him.

But the question can be raised, doesn't all religion demand "works? True but the distinction is "works because of righteousness" vs. "works of the religionist".

The religionist works to merit heaven, or be applauded, or to avoid being demoted or accused if they do nothing. These are just "works".

But the purified heart "works by love (Gal. 5). He is set to work out of a motivation sparked by a love for what the Savior has done for him. It energizes him like fire in the bones. The religionist can do many works, but he cannot do them by the principle of love—only a regenerated heart is capable of such action.

Fourth: A purified heart will result in an **Obedient Walk**

"Hereby we do know that we know him, if we keep his commandments. He that says, 'I know him,' and keeps not his commandments, is a liar, and the truth is not in him" (1 John 2:3,4). Make no mistake about it; Christ acknowledges none to be His disciples except those who do homage to Him as their Lord.

Too many religious "professors" pacify themselves with the idea that they possess imputed righteousness, while they are indifferent to the sanctifying work of the Spirit. They refuse to put on the garment of obedience, revealing their self-will, their enmity to God, and their non-submission to His Son.

Fifth: A Purified heart **Overcomes Temptations and Trials**

"For whatsoever is born of God overcomes the world: and this is the victory that overcomes the world, even our faith" (1 John 5:4). Notice that by the use of the present tense, the Apostle John is asserting that this is not just an ideal, which the true Believer strives for, but, in actuality, a reality he experiences in his life.

"Be of good cheer; I have overcome the world" (John 16:33). Christ overcame it for His people, and now He overcomes it in them. Through a purified heart, He opens our eyes to see the hollowness and worthlessness of the best which this world has to offer, and weans our hearts from it by satisfying them with spiritual things.

So little does the world attract the genuine child of God that he longs for the time to come when God shall take him out of it. Alas, that so very few of those now bearing the name of Christ have any real experimental acquaintance with these things. Alas, that so many are deceived by a faith, which is not a saving one.

Conclusion

These characteristics pose no threat for the one exercising true saving faith, since it becomes an opportunity for him to receive from the Lord, a validation of his Lord's acceptance of his faith. So, like the Psalmist, the one with the purified heart cries out, "Examine me, O Lord, and prove me; try my reins and my heart" (Psalm 26:2).

How does the real Christian differ from the religionist? This individual is filled with pride, and having a high opinion of himself. He is quite sure that Christ has saved him. He disdains any searching tests, and considers self-examination to be highly injurious and destructive of faith. He prefers preaching that keeps a respectable distance from his conscience, and elects to make no scrutiny of his heart. If you seek to convince him that his hope is a delusion, and his confidence presumptuous, he will regard you as an enemy, as Satan seeking to fill him with doubts. There is more hope of a murderer being saved than of his being disillusioned.

"He only is a Christian who lives for Christ. Many persons think it is enough to trust in Christ while they do not live for Him. But the Bible teaches us that if we are partakers of Christ's death, we are also partakers of His life. If we have any such appreciation of His love in dying for us as to lead us to confide in the merits of His death, we shall be constrained to consecrate our lives to His service. And this is the only evidence of the genuineness of our faith" (Charles Hodge on 2 Corinthians 5:15).

Reader, are the things mentioned above true of your own experience? If they are not, how worthless and wicked is your profession! Perhaps you are asking the question, "How can I obtain a genuine and saving faith"?

My answer is simple: if you desire to receive this gift, then you must put yourself in that way wherein He is willing to communicate it. Faith is the work of God, but He works it through the channels of His appointed means—instruments in His hands that He chooses to use to bring us to saving faith:

The first means is prayer. "A new heart also will I give you, and a new spirit will I put within you" (Ezekiel 36:26). So, cry earnestly to God for a new heart, for His regenerating Spirit, for the gift of saving faith.

The second means is the written Word, heard (John 17:20), or read (2 Timothy 3:15). The Scriptures are the Word of God; through them

Faith That Moves Mountains and Smashes Strongholds

He speaks. Then read them: asking Him to speak life, power, deliverance, and peace, to your heart.

Now that we have a clear idea of the faith that results in justification, we are ready to understand the faith that brings about sanctification. Here we will benefit from the writing of the Apostle James.

Chapter 10

Understanding the Relationship of Works to Faith

The grace that does not change my life will not save my soul. Charles Spurgeon

We have invested much ink describing the vital role that faith plays in obtaining "salvation full and free". We have learned that this precious gift of a loving God is appropriated by grace through the exercise of saving faith. It is a gift; therefore, not the result of any human efforts, called "works".

Now we are about to learn from James that while faith alone saves, the faith that saves is never alone; 'works' accompanies it.

The rectification of this apparent theological tug-of-war will occupy the attention of this chapter. We will share with you how a plan of salvation that permits no human effort (except repentance and the exercise of faith) to acquire it, nevertheless, insists on a vital role for works to verify it.

To appreciate this controversy, permit me to share verses from the Apostle Paul and the Apostle James that really look like the basis for a shouting match.

From the pen of Paul

- Romans 3:20, 28: *Therefore by the deeds of the law no flesh will be justified in His sight, for by the law is the knowledge of sin. . . . Therefore we conclude that a man is justified by faith apart from the deeds of the law.*
- Galatians 2:16: *. . . knowing that a man is not justified by the works of the law but by faith in Jesus Christ, even we have believed in Christ Jesus, that we might be justified by faith in Christ and not by the works of the law; for by the works of the law no flesh shall be justified;* and,
- Ephesians 2:8-9: *For by grace you have been saved through faith, and that not of yourselves; it is the gift of God, not of works, lest anyone should boast.*

From James Chapter 2
- 2:14: *What does it profit, my brethren, if someone says he has faith but does not have works? Can faith save him?*
- 2:18: *But someone will say: "You have faith and I have works". Show me your faith apart from your works, and I will show you my faith by my works."*
- 2:20–23: *Do you want to be shown, you foolish person, that faith apart from works is useless? Was not Abraham our father justified by works when he offered Isaac his son on the altar? You see that faith was working together with his works, and by works faith was made perfect.*
- 2:24: *You see then that a man is justified by works, and not <u>only</u> by faith only.*
- 2:25: *"And in the same way was not Rahab the prostitute justified by works when she received the messengers and sent them out by another way?*
- 2:26: *For as the body apart from the spirit is dead, so also faith apart from works is dead."*

How is it possible to rectify these two, seemingly, opposing viewpoints concerning the relationship of works to salvation? The answer, refreshing and illuminating, is possible through a careful analysis of the above verses in the Epistle of James. Once you grasp the true role of works in regard to salvation, you will find yourself motivated to walk more worthily.

Since Martin Luther's time, the second chapter of James has been a source of more theological firestorms than almost any other chapter or book of the Bible. Luther "re-discovered" the concept of true salvation as being "*sola fideles*" ("faith alone"). That phrase became the match that set Europe ablaze with revival.

Since he discovered the phrase (and the true Gospel) in the Book of Romans, Luther loved Romans. Then, he discovered the above verses in the Epistle of James and he wondered aloud how such concepts ever got into the Canon (authentic Bible) in the first place. But, with due respect to the great Reformer, the concepts that James discusses are very important to understanding the wider role of faith in Christian living.

Goal of this Chapter
Our goal in this chapter is to resolve this apparent contradiction through an expansive tour of the major components of the book; then an in depth analysis of the verses displayed above. When we are concluded you will wonder what all the fighting is about, and you will be able to evaluate the testimony of those who profess to know the Lord as their Savior. Hopefully, you will feel a touch of blessing as the presentation helps you to affirm, afresh, that you are truly a child of the King of Kings.

Where to Begin
As we approach this Epistle, we must first deal with who this author was, and then, who were his intended readers.

The Author

He was the half-brother of the Lord. His true name was "Jacob" (because he wrote the Letter in the Greek language he used the Greek equivalent of his name, "James".

The content of the book coincides with his public statements recorded in the Book of Acts (Acts 1:14; 12:17 etc.). Because of his piety, he became known as James the Just.

At the Crucifixion he was not a true believer; but became one thanks to a personal visit by the resurrected Lord—the only visit by the risen Lord to a non-believer. By AD 44 he had become a leader in the Jerusalem church (Acts 12:17).

Josephus says he was stoned after the death of Festus by the high priest and the Sadducees on a charge of transgressing the law. His ministry was primarily to the Jewish element that were forced to exit Jerusalem and moved eastward as a major Diasporas.

Surely a man who lived as a Nazarite (extreme Jewish legalism); and lost his life over the debate of Jewish vs. Christian works is qualified to speak on the subject, wouldn't you agree?

The Intended Audience

To whom did James write?

The very first lines provide us the answer:

James, a bondservant of God and of the Lord Jesus Christ, to the twelve tribes which are scattered abroad: Greetings" (James 1:1)

Clearly, they were Jewish people; followers of the Lord (regenerate, true Believers); and scattered abroad (who had to run for their lives under the onslaught of persecution.)

This Epistle is one of the earliest New Testament books to be written, probably ten years prior to Paul's Letters. James led a mega-congregation (several thousands) who became the target of Roman persecution. As a result they all had to exit their homes with only the clothes on their backs and the belongings they could stuff into their pockets. They became vagabonds, resettling hundreds of miles away (which were like thousands today).

James continues to track them, as a pastor with a scattered congregation. He then learns that they are being harassed in every possible manner. Their lives are actually brutal. In the pressure-cooker of their new life, they developed pressing theological questions:
- Am I genuinely saved?
- If I am saved by grace, and no works can be part of that process, then, by avoiding any works, I am okay?
- People have come into our new makeshift congregation and urged us to become involved in many works—some completely weird. What is the difference between good works and bad ones?

Understanding the Relationship of Works to Faith

Primarily, like church members on vacation, they started to drift away from the standards and practices that they had learned from James in their Jerusalem church. So he writes to straighten them out as well as answer tough questions concerning the balance between faith and works. In a nutshell, he shares two concepts: faith is essential to salvation, and works, in regard to salvation, it must never be used to secure a relationship with God that only grace can provide.

Bottom line, the most important thing for you to know about his intended readers is that James considered them saved people whom he cared for deeply. This becomes clear when you examine such passages as these:
- "*...Do not be deceived, my beloved <u>brethren.</u> 1:16);*
- *Of His own will He brought us forth by the word of truth, that <u>we</u> might be...*
- "*So then, <u>my beloved brethren</u>, let every man be swift to hear...*"

When you include the following four facts gained by research of the Letter it becomes clear that the audience was made of true believers that James had known and cared deeply about:
1. James 1:18 speaks of regeneration, using a term commonly associated with procreation, *brought forth*, hence an oblique reference to their being "born again".
2. The "you" implied in both 1:19 is connected to the "us" of verse 1:18.
3. His use of the affectionate title, *my beloved brethren* defines his use of "you".

So, clearly, in only these verses, we see whom James's readers were: born-again Jews scattered abroad.

Basis of James' Insistence on Works with Faith

In this Epistle James hammers on this subject of professing faith being accompanied by works so passionately. Why? I have discovered at least five reasons.

First, these are people indwelt by the Holy Spirit, therefore predisposed to receive and understand James' Spirit filled words. Unbelievers tend to consider works in two other ways. First they consider heaven to be earned by works (vs. grace), and make them essential to their hope. Second, they consider any warm feeling as qualifying as a good work. The true believer knows the fallacy of both of these false ideas. Only a true believer understands grace and its relationship to true (real) works.

Second, these true believers had, through trials and pain, already paid a huge price to be associated with Jesus. So their faith was not "Sunday religion"; it was the real deal—therefore, the balancing of true works with it was important for them to understand.

Third, their situation was so desperate that the only people they had to turn to for support, help and relief were those with whom they fellowshipped. James had to have realized this because he urges them to practice their good works by helping one another.

Fourth, every true Believer continually needs to learn, afresh, insights to help him grow in his walk. So, these readers would welcome his practical counsel.

Fifth: James understood what a powerful witness would result from these readers practicing acts of kindness and selflessness (works) in the midst of an impossible situation. It would be the one thing the false believers could not do because such actions require the power of the Holy Spirit to pull off.

Now that we understand his intended audience, we are ready to understand the intended meaning of his message.

Analysis of the Message of James 2

Before we tackle this very important chapter, let me share how it fits into the Epistle. To guide your thinking in this fashion I need to share with you, briefly, the process by which we arrive at an understanding of its intended meaning.

A Word about Textual Analysis

The message of any New Testament Epistle is constructed according to a logical order, beginning with the smallest unit of sense (sentences) that are combined into units of meaning (paragraphs), which, in turn, are

Understanding the Relationship of Works to Faith

organized into units of argument. By summarizing all of the major units of argument, we know what the intended message of the Book connected into units of argument (sections), which in turn, connected to form stand-alone message of what the Book is.

So, then expressing the intended meaning of a chapter comes by first understanding the message of the Book (by the above process) and then applying the over-arching theme as a sort of North Star to make sure your analysis of the words, sentences, and paragraphs of James chapter two fit the over-all point of the Epistle. Okay, I just gave you Hermeneutics 101, but it was a major part of the academic studies I completed for my Doctor of Ministry degree.

So we will first analyze the Book of James as a background to uncovering the meaning of the key paragraph that deals with faith and works of faith. Bottom line, it was written to urge them to embrace the absolute necessity of affirming their professed faith with accompanying good works. James even goes so far as to say, without works, your faith is actually worthless.

Wouldn't it be great if James outlined this sermon as we preachers in Trinidad are taught who use *western* type logic (thinking)? This approach (actually invented by Aristotle) follows this blueprint. Such "westernized" sermons begin with an opening statement, followed by a propositional statement. This proposition is then developed, in detail with two or three (or more) key supporting arguments. This type of sermon then closes with a final appeal to action.

But James possessed a mind that was eastern in thinking. He follows a topical approach that is not as tightly structured. The eastern type of sermonic structure can seem to meander. This difference is frustrating to scholars schooled in western style sermon structuring. Martin Dibelius declared that he found no logical plan; and concluded that the Epistle's chief characteristic was its *lack of continuity*. My approach to the Letter is to focus on five topical themes that coincide with our modern chapter divisions. They are connected with a common thread resembling a string of pearls.

I discovered the thread that ties each topical section together into a cohesive "whole" by combining two verses that represent the two major ideas he brings together:

- Idea One: James 1:2: "Count it all joy, my brothers, when you meet trials of various kinds, for you know that the testing of your faith produces steadfastness. And let steadfastness have its full effect, that you may be perfect and complete, lacking in nothing."
- Idea Two: is expressed by combining two verses: "What does it profit, my brethren, if someone says he has faith but does not have works? Can faith save him? (2:14); and "… *as the body apart from the spirit is dead, so also faith apart from works is dead." (2:26)*

So the Big Picture emerges: James writes to encourage these true believers to view the inevitable tribulation they were suffering so as to see how it could become something beneficial. But in order to tap into the blessings from the Holy Spirit they must act on the things they professed to believe. Such acts of kindness and ministry were absolutely essential. To be unable or unwilling to combine works with faith was proof that the profession was phony.

Although this Letter breaks into five major topics, I am going to appeal to your "western mindset" by blending them into a westernized outline.

Outline of James

1. Prologue (1:2–18)

Here James speaks to the issue of the trials that the Believers were facing. He deals with the external and internal sources of trials, and counsels them as to the necessity to maintain eternal vigilance to walk by faith. He advised them that reaction to trial, if handled properly (i.e. with faith combined with works) could produce wonderful "side benefits", including, having their profession of faith validated as real; growing (maturing), and learning to seek God for everything, thereby "lacking nothing".

2. Thematic Statement (1:19)

Out of the many, we have chosen this primary admonition: "Be doers of the Word and not hearers only, deceiving yourselves." Trusting in the Word and acting on it distinguishes true religion (faith-walk), from the false variety (faith based on beliefs inconsistent with the Word, and producing either no works or bad works). This type of faith James calls "pure religion" i.e., the kind that God approves and blesses.

3. Body of the Epistle (1:21-5:6)
In this major section, James deals with three major topics:
- Faith Tested by Works (chapter 2)
  He argues that faith without love or accompanying works is dead.
- Faith Tested by Words (chapter 3
  James argues that words matter and he lays out rules and roles for the tongue, i.e., how one uses speech in social situations.
- Faith tested by Worldliness (chapter 4:1 -5:6)
  He probes beneath the surface of trials to show their demonic source, their Divine solution, and the deceitful character of worldliness.

Actually, in a sentence in chapter one, James provides the three topics in summary. Using a characteristic introductory phrase, (*"Let every man be..."*):
- James 1:21 – 2:26 "Let everyone be SWIFT TO HEAR
- James 3:1-18 "Let everyone be SLOW TO SPEAK, and
- James 4:1 – 5:6 "Let everyone be SLOW TO WRATH

With this larger perspective in mind, we will now focus on the final topic that is imbedded in the Closing we will call an Epilogue.

4. Epilogue (5:7–20).
James concludes the book offering counsel that instructs the people about how faith must be tested by watchfulness, especially offering counsel concerning riches, oppression, and holy living.

With this overall understanding, let us now sharpen our focus on Chapter two, the section that urges us to be "Swift to Hear".

Understanding the "Swift to Hear" Section (chapter two)

When his readers heard the above phrase *"Swift to Hear"*, they were programmed to immediately connect hearing with obeying. Their Hebrew word for "hear" means "to obey". The chapter falls nicely into two main Parts:

1. The first one argues that faith without love is dead (2:1-13). It deals with an example of bad faith, i.e. the kind that results in bad works.
2. The second section argues that faith without works is dead (2:14-26). It includes a bad example (demonic faith), followed by two examples of faith plus works; followed by an analogy that perfectly summarizes his theme.

The chapter is a sermonic presentation of this principle:

Part One Analysis (2:1 – 13)

This section revolves around the opening expression, "Show no partiality as you hold the faith of our Lord Jesus Christ, the Lord of Glory". . The foremost issue is about works, and the worst kind is a work you do for personal benefit instead of for the Lord's glory. James said the consequence is that at the judgment for works, when you need mercy, you will receive not because you failed to show mercy in your life.

The reason is, says James, you will face a judgment for your works, and if you fail to show mercy (the right kind of work), then, at the judgment of the believers (where works are to be judged) you will not receive mercy from the Lord.

Also, James uses a special description for the Lord Jesus: "our Lord Jesus Christ, the Lord of Glory". The last phrase connects the Jesus of the Gospel with the Shekinah Glory of Israel in the wilderness. The symbolism is fascinating in its relevance. This guiding Cloud was comprised of an invisible reality (that only God could see) and a practical, visible exterior—the light and cloud. I see it as an analogy for faith and works in combination. The internal portion—profession—which only God can know as real, is combined with a practical visible, exterior—works to create— something beneficial to all, and glorifying to God. The same analogy holds for Jesus Himself; He visibly manifested the spiritual reality of the Father, as works do for faith.

Next James describes a situation that will serve as an example of bad works. Showing partiality was more pronounced in their day because all barriers based on income, status, and race were very defined. But Jesus, by His resurrection smashed all such barriers for His own people. Therefore, to attempt to resurrect such favoritism was evil—because it shows the reason for such actions—to curry factor for one's own benefit.

Showing partiality to wealthy individuals is especially dangerous for three reasons. First, it builds a false concept of the basis for God's blessing (wealth = blessing). Second, it causes a sinner to miss the mind of God (who judges not by outward appearance). Finally, such actions provoke people to start choosing the commandments they will obey, mainly based on their own self-interests.

Having built the case that faith without works leads to loveless, self-centered religion, James will now zero in on this principle: faith that does not result in works is dead.

Part Two Analysis: 2:14 - 26

Part One deals with the relationship between works and faith on a social level. Part Two deals with the relationship between work and faith on a theological basis.

In Part One James contended that if faith does not produce tangible acts of kindness and mercy, then it lacks love. In this second Part he contends that *true faith will be tested by works; if it fails to produce works, it is dead.*

The section is developed by three examples, each accompanied by statements which declare certain principles relevant to his argument. He then sums up his entire argument in a final analogy. We shall now describe and comment on each of these four main sections of Part Two.

> First principle
> "*What does it profit, my brethren, if someone says he has faith but does not have works. Can faith save him?*" (2:14)

This sentence actually continues the question raised in 2:1 regarding a faith "professor" being confronted with a genuine need, fails to respond with tangible action.

To appreciate the power of this statement, permit me to shed light on the meanings of the key words in this sentence:

- "Profit" (ορφελλω) The word means, "increase", "advantage", or improvement in the quality and quantity of one's life. This worthlessness is twofold, as we shall see shortly.
- "If": This structure tells you that the question is considered rhetorical; that the answer is, "of course not".
- "Works": (εργον) The word means:
  1. Any activity in which one expends energy, time, and perspiration.
  2. Any product generated by human effort;
  3. Any deed accomplished by personal involvement.

So, without doubt, work is tangible, measurable, handmade, and requires energy (sweat) to be expended.

With these brief word studies, we can now see how all of this relates to faith. Bad faith produces no work, no tangible action. This is the very kind of faith that the demons exhibit. It can be described in one word—"dead" νςεκροσ, which James likens to physical death when a person's spirit vacates their body; and all that remains is to mourn and bury them.

A sustained absence of breath confirms that the physical body is deceased. Likewise, if the works which living faith produces have no existence, it is a proof that faith itself (literally, 'in respect to itself') has no existence.

To illustrate this principle, James offers another example that mirrors the one he presented in Part One. Here he puts these words in a person with a dead faith because it produces not tangible help. After sizing up a person hungry and freezing, it says, "Be warmed and filled". These words are telling because they reveal that the person (demonstrating bad faith) knew the extent of the destitution of the people he addresses, but did not desire to provide any help except a few religious words.

This bad example was designed to showcase genuine faith, since it is always accompanied by tangible, practical help (works). Bad faith neither helps the destitute person, nor triggers God's blessing reserved for true faith responses.

James then hammers home the point of this chapter: show ("exhibit) your works; otherwise we know your profession of faith is phony. Bottom line, genuine faith must be accompanied by tangible help.

Next, James wants to make very clear what he means by dead faith. There is no better example than that exemplified by the demons.

Example of Dead Faith: Demons

The demons exemplify dead faith. They believe in God's existence; but, instead of responding in faith, they respond with fear and trembling. This word "tremble (i.e. abject fear)" means the demons shudder because they know that they are facing the pure and complete wrath in divine judgment—without any hope of salvation. Therefore, the illegitimacy of their faith is proven by their tangible response.

After presenting two bad examples (church members showing preferential treatment to the wealthy, and demons) James presents two examples of genuine faith.

The principle that he will seek to illustrate occurs in these three verses:

> *Do you want to be shown, you foolish person, that faith apart from works is useless? Was not Abraham our father justified by works when he offered Isaac his son on the altar? You see that faith was working together with his works, and by works faith was made perfect. 2:20–23:*

Notice a key word, "fool". Its Greek word is κενασ. It represent the idea of a foolish or vain, i.e., devoid of truth. Metaphorically, it means " destitute, yet boasting of spiritual wealth; but devoid of any supporting evidence".

To this person, James offers two perfect examples of faith accompanied by works, Abraham and Rahab.

Example of Excellence: Abraham

From our previous discussions of Abraham, we focused on the fact that he was justified by faith decades before he trudged up Mt. Moriah to sacrifice Isaac. James describes him as "righteous"., i.e., "justified" when used in connection to God. It implies two things:
  i) God declared him righteous by his work of faith) and,

ii) He was put right before God by his actions.

If you recall the actual statement of Gen. 22:12 in this context, you will find these words spoken by God: "Now I know that you fear God".

Notice that James says that Abraham was justified because of what he did:

> "*Because Abraham truly trusted in God, God considered that he was righteous*" (James 2:23a). James makes this point: Abraham was the father of our faith *because of what he **did**.. In his mind, he laid the boy on that altar with the settled conviction that the boy was as good as dead.*

In Abraham's mind the offering was a settled, completed action; the boy, whose hand he held as they trudged up the mountain was, in Abraham's mind, as good as dead.

The genuineness of his faith is proven by his reward, which is described, "*...and he was called the friend of God*". Two key words reveal much insight into the extent of his reward for a work of faith: "*Called*" (*kaleo*) means to receive a title; and "*friend*" refers to a relationship so close and personal that intimate secrets and deep personal concerns are exchanged.

To James, Abraham's work was so vital to his salvation that the act of obedience completed his faith. It became the basis for James' principle: the only kind of faith that justifies, is that which is accompanied by works, since works are the only viable way to demonstrate that the person exercising faith (i.e. believer) is actually a regenerated person. In this he agrees with Paul (2 Corinthians 5:17).

But we must be very clear. The expression, *Abraham . . . justified by works*" must be put into context. Certainly, by his works, he was not justified before God. But, before men (the watching world) his works served as "evidentiary justification. His faith, first declared when he left Ur to venture out to "a city whose builder and maker were God", was genuine. I know this is so, because, years later, when he stood before Isaac with the knife in hand, it was proven to be genuine, i.e. proven to be authentic (just) by his works. In the way James uses the word "justified", you could substitute the word "validated".. How do the two concepts of justification make sense? This simple illustration will make it all clear.

Before it ever produces any fruit, an apple tree affirmed that it was such a tree. God knew that it was a tree capable of producing apples. But when the first apple hit the ground, the tree's "profession" was confirmed. The fruit legitimized its claim to be an apple tree. Likewise, works confirm (justify) the claim to possess faith.

Another Good Example of Faith: Rahab

> 2:25: *"And in the same way was not Rahab the prostitute justified by works when she received the messengers and sent them out by another way?*

For his next illustration of this principle, James turns to another person we have already discussed—Rahab. We need only mention her because her faith, being justified by work, so mirrors that of Abraham that we would be repeating our self.

You will recall that she embraced the God of Israel as her Savior and demonstrated her trust in Him by hiding the spies and seeking salvation from their God. Notice that she believed, but then, here faith caused her to do something. Would her faith have saved her if she had not acted on that faith? Hardly. The spies even told her this would be the case.

Before I move on to the final analogy, permit me to make a final essential point about these two excellent Biblical examples of true faith. Together they offer these insights about the vital connection between faith and accompanying good works. From Abraham's example we can learn this principle: if we believe in God, we will do what He tells us to do. The lesson from Rahab is also clear: if we believe in God, we will help His people, even at our own expense. As Abraham gave up his son, so Rahab gave up her family. The final analogy will pull it all together with total clarity.

Final Example: an Analogy

James adds one final statement to summarize all he has said about the relationship of faith and works: "For as the body apart from the spirit is dead, so also faith apart from works is dead." (2:26).

The first word, "for" (γαρ) alerts you that James is about to pull all of chapter two together for one final summarizing statement. Think of this as saying, *"I said all that to say this…"*

Again, we return to the analogy introduced earlier in this chapter: a living human body vs. a dead one, as analogous to a living (real) faith and a dead (phony) faith. However, in this final analogy, we are greeted with a dramatic "twist".

Notice the analogy: the physical body is connected to faith. The "breath" is compared to works. Since faith is invisible, it should follow that it be compared to breath (since both are invisible). Likewise work and the physical body should be comparable since both are visible.

However, by reversing these comparisons, James stresses the fact that works are the life-giving force (breath) to faith. It is his way of highlighting the point of his argument: Works are the life force of faith so much so that without them, faith is graveyard dead.

Is it possible to have a faith with no works? It is as impossible as trying to live without having any breath in your lungs. Within minutes you will become a corpse!

What Does Faith without Works Mean?

Kistemaker expresses this viewpoint: "A faith that is void of deeds is not genuine and is therefore completely different from faith committed to Christ." The logic yields what will henceforth be called the Subtraction Model. It conceives of the word *"without"* as implying that *faith without works* as referring to something less than *faith*. Kistemaker call this viewpoint the Subtraction Model.

The Subtraction Model

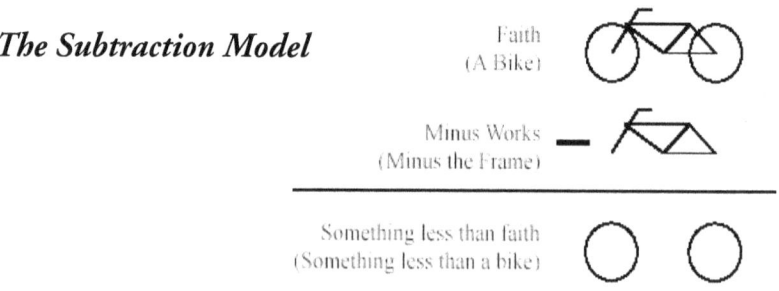

Faith (A Bike)
Minus Works (Minus the Frame)
Something less than faith (Something less than a bike)

Understanding the Relationship of Works to Faith

For Kistemaker, *faith without works* is something less than faith. He would understand James to use the word *faith* to describe something that does not really qualify as faith.

To appreciate how faith and works must work together, consider the operation of a bicycle. If it only has a frame, it cannot be considered a real bicycle. A frameless bicycle is like sanctifying faith without accompanying works.

Like the bicycle, sanctifying faith must contain faith and works operating in balance and tandem. To fail to connect the two concepts, i.e., as the Subtraction Model does, is something less than what James intended.

Think of sanctifying faith as "phase two" faith. It must not be confused with "phase one" faith, justifying faith. This is the mistake that many Bible commentators make.

Regeneration results from faith alone in Christ by grace alone. James reminded those regenerate people that what they now needed to be saved from was the deadly power of sin (James 1:21), which ruins their walk with Christ.

This type of deliverance could only result from understanding the truth of the Bible, then applying it by faith to one's own personal experience, and then, as a result, obeying what the Word said to do.

These steps are the work that must accompany sanctifying faith.

If the Subtraction Model fails to properly reflect the meaning of sanctifying faith, is there another model? It is called the Addition Model.

The Addition Model

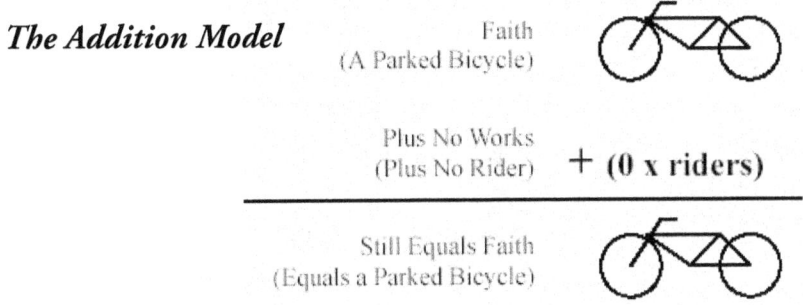

Faith
(A Parked Bicycle)

Plus No Works
(Plus No Rider) **+ (0 x riders)**

Still Equals Faith
(Equals a Parked Bicycle)

Keep in mind that the Addition Model only applies to born-again believers (people possessing Christ's perfect eternal life). Just like a bicycle without a rider is still a bicycle, *faith without* works is still *faith*.

Does the Addition Model of phase-two deliverance fit the passage? Yes, it does! James warns these believers that they must apply the word (which they believe) to receive any phase-two deliverance from the deadly power of sin in their Christian lives. Only by taking in and applying the Word could the *beloved brethren* (believers) be delivered from a wholesale experience of divine discipline, even including the sin unto death.

In his book *I Surrender,* Patrick Morley writes that the church's integrity problem is in the misconception "that we can add Christ to our lives, but not subtract sin. It is a change in belief without a change in behavior." He goes on to say, "It is revival without reformation, without repentance." As we have seen, it requires both subtraction and addition.

Resolving the Initial Question of Works: James vs. Paul

Now that we have analyzed the interconnection between faith and works, we shall conclude this chapter by answering the question with which we began: Does James contradict Paul's words in Romans 4:1-10, especially where he talks about the faith of Abraham.

Doctrinal Foundation of the Controversy

Make no mistake about it; faith and works can be opposite and irreconcilable.

If God "justifies the ungodly," works cannot be, in any sense or to any degree, the ground of justification. For this reason man's only legitimate response is to reject any hope placed in his self-efforts, and rush to "believe in Him who has that justifying righteousness to bestow on the ungodly penitent who acknowledges that he deserves none of it but embraces it.

Since Paul advocates salvation by grace through faith without works; and James argues that faith and works are interconnected, is this real or imagined debate?

This alleged controversy could be resolved when you understand two important concepts. The first is a concept that describes how both apostles, operating with a Hebrew's mindset, processed information; it is a concept called "Semitic Totality. Second, when you understand the perspective of each apostle regarding Abraham's salvation, you will see that no conflict existed.

We will now describe each of these issues and relate how each resolves the apparent controversy.

Semitic Totality

Semitic Totality is part of the Hebrew worldview. It is a way of processing concepts. It never varies.

Regarding faith, this concept insists that if one's faith is genuine, it will always result in works. Consider this definition: the Semitic Totality Concept means that "a man's thoughts form one totality with their results in action so that 'thoughts' that result in no action are 'vain'."

Applied to the role of works following faith, this means that there can be no decision without corresponding action, for the total person will inevitably reflect a choice that is made. Thought and action are linked under the Semitic Totality paradigm.

Thus, what we would consider separate actions of conversion, confession, and obedience in the form of works would be considered by the Hebrews to be an act in totality. "Both the act and the meaning of the act mattered -- the two formed for the first Christians an indivisible unity.

You see this principle working in James when he insists that without works, faith is dead; and when he labels people with dead faith as "vain". Likewise, it emerges from the numerous admonitions of Paul to believers to realize their position in Christ and behave accordingly. When Paul encourages believers to "work out your own salvation with fear and trembling," (Phil. 2:12) he is not telling them that they must do their part to be saved. They already possess that righteousness. What is needed is for them to come to terms with this and live consistently with it.

Both Apostles then apply the concept of Semitic Totality when they agree that someone who does not do works clearly has no faith to speak of, none that is living. Paul's admonitions to good behavior would find a matching sentiment than James 1:22-24. This passage, expresses the principle in Semitic Totality that "hearers" who are not "doers" are deceiving themselves, not knowing what they are really like, just like the "man in the mirror" does not know his own appearance.

Abraham's Salvation: Two Perspectives

The discussion of Abraham as a model for each of their views sparked the debate. Ironically it will also provide the resolution of it.

To begin, you need to understand that both apostles quote Gen. 15:6 (as stated at the outset of this chapter). Also, both agreed that Abraham had been justified by faith. Where they seemed to disagree was in the next step—the sacrifice of Isaac. Paul views it as an act of faith. James focuses on it as an act of obedience. In fact, the sacrifice was both.

By focusing upon Isaac's sacrifice as an act of faith, Paul will use it to instruct on the doctrine of justification. James, by viewing the same sacrifice as an act of obedience draws our attention to the doctrine of sanctification.

The resolution draws even nearer when you understand who each apostle was speaking to. Paul spoke to unregenerate minds that needed to be saved. James addressed regenerate minds that needed their faith validated

The resolution becomes complete when you understand the type of works they connected with true faith. Paul showed that Abraham's salvation was validated by his circumcision. This work was designed, as an act of obedience; to show that in placing his faith in God, he had cut himself off from any hope in human or self-help (symbolized by flesh).

James never even mentions circumcision; that spiritual work had already been accomplished (e.g., by baptism). Instead his works are acts that only a regenerate heart can conceive and execute: acts of mercy, kindness, obedience to the Word, and serving people without discrimination

So the controversy is resolved. True faith can never be detached from visible work. Paul's focus on Abraham was that he (Abraham) was justified solely according to his faith. The proper label for the aspect of Abraham's salvation that Paul deals with is called Justification, an *objective,* not a *subjective* change--a change from guilt and condemnation to acquittal

Understanding the Relationship of Works to Faith

and acceptance. The proper label for James' doctrinal focus is called Sanctification—a subjective change from dead faith to living faith

In fact, when James' says that Abraham was justified by *such* a work he was, in fact agreeing with Paul when he insisted that Abraham's faith was expressed in action.

Paul uses Abraham's action in the sacrifice of Isaac as an example of faith; while James uses it as evidence of the validity of the man's faith. The works of the law that Paul condemns are completely different from the works of faith, which James advocates.

Bottom line, both men looked at the same act of faith from two different perspectives. No controversy exists, as Abraham became justified *before the world* as righteous through faith manifested in words and works.

His commandments. Those who live in rebellion and who ignore the Word of God demonstrate that they do not possess true saving faith, that they are deceiving themselves. They have dead faith, not saving faith.

Also, the two apostles address different issues. Paul is teaching justification over and against specific observation of the Jewish law, such as circumcision (Rom. 3:1), and doing so with reference to a person *prior to* conversion.

James is advocating the practical outworking of faith (i.e. validation) through generally moral behavior, but not through anything uniquely associated with the Jewish law, and *after conversion*.

As is often the case, critics seeking rivalry are missing the forest for the trees.

Henry Alford wrote, "We are all justified." This includes:
- Justified judicially by God (Rom 8:33);
- Justified meritoriously, by Christ (Isa. 53:11);
- Justified mediatorily, by faith (Rom 5:1); and,
- Justified evidentially, by works.

Paul's discussion of Abraham's justification is judicial, meritorious, and mediatorily. James' reference to Abraham's justification is the evidential variety.

So, tonight, dear reader, you can go to bed and rest, assured that the "rhubarb" between Paul's concept of faith and that of James does not exist.

Conclusion

The issue of faith and works is a microcosm of a larger issue—demonstrating the validity of the truth of the Scriptures using dogmatic truth (words) and empirical evidence (works). Let me explain.

Christianity is unique among belief systems in that its dogmatic truth is backed up with empirical evidence, which includes fulfilled prophecy, and the resurrection. I submit that works serve as the empirical support for the dogmatic truth regarding justification. Surely James could be summed up in this bumper-sticker expression: *Faith alone saves, but the faith that saves is not alone*

Founder of the Salvation Army, William Booth beautifully expressed the point of James Chapter two: "Faith and works should travel side by side, step answering to step, like the legs of men walking. First faith, and then works; and then faith again, and then works again -- until they can scarcely distinguish which is the one and which is the other."

A young boy, on an errand for his mother, had just bought a dozen eggs. Walking out of the store, he tripped and dropped the sack. All the eggs broke, and the sidewalk was a mess. The boy tried not to cry. A few people gathered to see if he was OK and to tell him how sorry they were. In the midst of the works of pity, one man handed the boy a quarter. Then he turned to the group and said, "I care 25 cents worth. How much do the rest of you care?" James would concur: words don't mean much if we have the ability to do more; i.e. to produce the kind of works that show that we care "that much".

Chapter 11

Secret to Mountain Moving Faith: God's Faithfulness

Missionary statesman Hudson Taylor had complete trust in God's faithfulness. In his journal he wrote:

> *"Our heavenly Father is a very experienced One. He knows very well that His children wake up with a good appetite every morning...He sustained 3 million Israelites in the wilderness for 40 years. We do not expect He will send 3 million missionaries to China; but if He did, He would have ample means to sustain them all...Depend on it, God's work done in God's way will never lack God's supply."*

Hudson Taylor, after years of missionary work in China felt that God was calling him to plant missionaries in the inland part of China with a vast population, and not a single Gospel witness.

At his death, Taylor left behind a flourishing ministry, China Inland Mission, supporting over one thousand trained missionaries serving the Lord.

He was once asked to explain the source of such effective ministry. He turned to this New Testament passage:

Faith That Moves Mountains and Smashes Strongholds

> "And Jesus answering, said unto them,' Have faith in God'. For verily I say unto you, that whosoever shall say unto this mountain, 'Be thou removed, and be thou cast into the sea; and shall not doubt in his heart, but shall believe that those things which he says shall come to pass; he shall have whatsoever he says. Therefore I say unto you, whatsoever things you desire, when ye pray, believe that ye receive them, and ye shall have them." (Mark 11:22-24).

So, we come to the last stop on our journey. Ironically, we return to the question that launched this discussion: What kind of faith can cause a mountain just not to shudder, or shake (an earthquake) but actually MOVE?

Hudson Taylor was asked by a group of visiting pastors to share with them what he felt to be the key that enabled him to exert the sufficient faith to build his expansive missionary organization.

Taylor replied, "I reckon on God's faithfulness and embrace the idea as a deep conviction that what had been true for Abraham would be equally valid for my own ministry." He went on. "This idea actually occurs in Hebrews, '…He (Abraham) believed in the Lord and it was counted to him for righteousness'." One of the preachers later remarked, "My, what a simple, pure faith the man possessed!"

We have probed Abraham's faith at length. His faith is discussed not just in the Old Testament but also in the Gospels, as well as the Epistles of Paul and James. We will not discuss it further. But there is one final aspect of faith that we need to acquaint you with, dear reader. It is behind every step of faith, whether it be Abraham's or yours. I invite you to consider the one thing that makes faith even possible—the faithfulness of God. All mountain moving faith counts on one thing: it "reckons" on the God keeping His Word to us, in our day and predicament, just as to Abraham. Understanding it will do for your life and ministry as it served Hudson Taylor in his, and later, to his son, James, who assumed the reins of leadership at his father's death.

The Board overseeing the leadership, with James Taylor, of China Inland Mission, fell into a common problem of second-generation ministries. They reveled and extolled the faith of those who built the Mission in "yesteryear". But each ministry opportunity James presented was met with reluctance. It appeared to be serious minded caution. In truth, it was largely based on unbelief. They had failed to consider that the power of God available to the founder would also be available to support the son's leadership.

As soon as James would present a new idea for reaching the lost, the Board would gently interject, "What would your father do?" Among the many implications, this one will suffice: "Don't rock the boat, son. Stay with the vision your father began". But James Taylor felt that the Mission needed to move forward to a new day beyond the one his father had even have contemplated.

For months James pondered how to deal with this negative spirit among the leadership. Then when meditating on the verse, "He is the same yesterday, today and forever." (Heb. 13:8) a strategy came to mind.

The next morning when these people came into his office they found that he had placed on the wall behind his chair these words framed as painting, "***...and today...***"

How that blesses me—to be confronted with the fresh precious truth that the power of God to respond to a person of faith is just as available today as it ever was.

If all of the Old Testament was built upon a covenant relationship with the living Lord, then His faithfulness has to be a primary attribute in His keeping this covenant promises. As you read the "older covenant" (the New Testament is a new covenant in His blood), you discover that Jehovah is often referred to as *"**the faithful God**"*. . To appreciate this check out these verses:

- "Know therefore that the Lord thy God, he is God, *the faithful God*, which keeps covenant and mercy with them that love and keep His commandments to a thousand generations. (Deut. 7:9. (Note: 1000 years is certainly faithful enough for anyone, yet it was only a hyperbole, and actually signified, the indefinite time in the future, i.e. forever.)
- "Thus says the Lord, the Redeemer of Israel, and his Holy One to him whom man despises, to him whom the nations abhors, to a servant of rulers, kings shall see and arise, princes also shall worship, because of *the Lord that is faithful* and the Holy One of Israel, and he shall choose thee (Is. 49:7).

In each of these verses we find the word "faithful". What light can a word study shed on its meaning?

Faith That Moves Mountains and Smashes Strongholds

Meaning of the Word "Faithful"

In the Old Testament, the Hebrew word enjoyed a fascinating history. The root meaning suggests the ideas of "propping up" or "supporting". When in reference to another person it means "one in whom you may completely lean upon, i.e. put your full weight upon". How that blesses me!

A famous Scottish preacher was going out to counsel a woman who had requested him since she wanted to "get faith" (her words). As the man approached her country home he had to cross a stream where she had erected a very impromptu bridge.

As the minister looked at the thin plank, she cried out to him (in a strong Scottish dialect), "Jist lippen to it". These words are not misspelled. They were native to her Scot language. More importantly, they were her way of advising the preacher to not fear the bridge caving in, but to just trust himself to the wooden planks to support his weight.

As he shared with her about the way of salvation, he searched for a word to explain saving faith. Suddenly, recalling her words, he said "Jist lippen to Him"! Her eyes brightened as she realized that the promises of Jesus regarding her eternal soul could support her faith and even the lingering doubt she carried. Understanding the faithfulness of God brought that woman to faith. It would then become the centerpiece of her trust and hope as she looked to Him to meet her needs each day in every way.

Also, do not forget how the faithfulness of God manifested itself to the pastor. Enroute, he had asked the Lord for the right words to share that would turn her heart to repentance; and in a moment of panic, the Lord had provided exactly what the man needed and requested to accomplish the task.

New Testament Aspects of Meaning

The Greek word for "faithfulness" conveys the idea of "being trustworthy", or "totally reliable". As you can see, this word is completely interchangeable with the Hebrew counterpart.

So, whether in the language of the Old or the New Testament, the word "faithfulness" is defined as a state where we are able to absolutely rely or "stay" (i.e., put the entire weight of your need or your hope) yourself on a person or object.).

Surely this aspect of faith we desperately need to understand; especially in this day where unfaithfulness dominates our business dealings, and marital infidelity abounds. In fact, the times make the subject all the more appealing to us all.

How refreshing, then, how unspeakably blessed, to lift our eyes above the situation in which we all live, to behold He who *is* faithful, faithful in all things, faithful at all times.

"Know therefore that the Lord thy God, He is God, the *faithful* God" (Deut. 7:9). This quality is essential to His being, without it He would not be God. For God to be unfaithful would be to act contrary to His nature, which were impossible: "If we believe not, yet He abideth faithful; He cannot deny Himself" (2 Tim. 2:13).

Faithfulness is one of the glorious perfections of His being. God is, so to speak, clothed in faithfulness: "O Lord God of hosts, who is a strong Lord like unto Thee; or to Thy faithfulness *round about* Thee?" (Ps. 89:8).

What a word is that in Psalm 36:5, Thy mercy, "O Lord, is in the heavens; and Thy faithfulness unto the clouds." Far above all finite comprehension is the unchanging faithfulness of God. Everything about God is great, vast, and incomparable. He never forgets, never fails, never falters, and never forfeits His word. He adheres to every word of every promise or prophecy. "God is not a man, that He should lie; neither the son of man, that He should repent: hath He said, and shall He not do it? Or hath He spoken, and shall He not make it good?" (Num. 23:19). Therefore, our trusting hearts can know that "His compassions fail not, they are new every morning: *great* is Thy faithfulness" (Lam. 3:22, 23).

Throughout the pages of every Book, you will find God's faithfulness being illustrated. How can it be otherwise? The Bible is about God in all His glory and grace and God is true. The promises of His Word are rock solid sure. His dealing with people in the Bible demonstrates the perfect consistency of His faithfulness. The reason is simple; faithfulness is a central attribute of His nature. He is, in His faithfulness, simply "being Himself".

If you hunger to really know this, then there is only one way. The key to being able to discern His faithfulness is to act upon His promises. Action turns expectancy into reality. In taking the step to trust Him and then act upon it, you discover that "He is *faithful* that promised" (Heb. 10:23).

Of course there are seasons in our lives when it is not easy, for even the best of us practicing Christians, to believe that God *is* faithful. In such moments, our faith gets hammered and tested to the point we can no longer see His loving kindness or sense His Presence. We all know of these times don't we—when plans have been smashed and friends have betrayed us. We stumble. We cry out, "Oh Lord where are You when I am hurting so much?"

If this expresses your heart, savor, like cool water on a burning tongue, these wonderful words: "Who is among you that fears the Lord, that obeys the voice of His servant, that walks in darkness and hath no light? Let him trust in the name of the Lord, and *stay upon his God*." (Isaiah 50:10). I love the point of this precious truth: when there is nothing left to trust, you CAN trust the faithfulness of the Lord!

Paul was resting on the faithfulness of God when he said, I know whom I have believed, and am persuaded that He is able to keep that which I have committed unto Him against that day (2 Tim 1:12).

I share this truth in order to help reverse any worry that problems have caused, and also to preserve you from its choke hold if you are currently "between worries." Consider the faithfulness of the One Job is referring to when he wrote, "He *shall* deliver thee in six troubles: yea, in seven there shall be no evil touch thee." Job 5:19.

When you focus on His faithfulness, three things occur. First, the tendency to complain and grumble is diminished. Second, God is honored by the fact that in the midst of your pain, you recognize and acknowledge His love and faithfulness. Third, such thoughts will serve to strengthen the confidence you have in God. Peter had this in mind when he wrote, "Wherefore let them that suffer according to the will of God commit the keeping of their souls to Him in well to Him in well doing, as unto a faithful Creator" (1 Pet. 4:19)

But what do we do when we reckon on the faithfulness of God? Let us explore the following.

What to Reckon On God to Provide

Now, permit me to provide you, dear reader, with some very practical counsel as to specific areas in which you can reckon on God's faithfulness.

We are now ready to pull all of these thoughts together, to consider some important applications to the principle. I will mention, briefly, only these areas

Reckon on God's Faithfulness to Deliver You from Trials

This means to reckon on His unfailing defense and deliverance of His servants in times of trial, testing and conflict, God proves His faithfulness as these verses declare:
- "It is of the Lord' mercies that we are not consumed, because his compassion fail not. They are new every morning; great is Thy faithfulness (Lam. 3:22-23).
- "For Israel hath not been forsaken, nor Judah or His God, of the Lord of hosts; though their land was filled with sin against the Holy One of Israel." (Jer. 51:5).

Also, you can reckon on His faithfulness to stand with His children, and save them when they are going through the worst types of circumstances. To encourage you I share this promise, "If we are faithless, he abides faithful for he cannot deny himself." (2 Tim. 2:13)

Reckon on God's Faithfulness to Deliver You from Sin's Temptation

God demonstrates His faithfulness by the way in which He does not allow His children to be tempted above that which they are able, but with the temptation, makes a way of escape so that they may be able to bear up under it. This truth is attested to as these verses declare:
- "Go is faithful, who will not suffer you to be tempted above that ye are able; but will with the temptation make a way to escape, that ye may be able to bear it." (I Cor. 10:13).
- "But the Lord is faithful, who shall establish you, and guard you from the evil one." (2 Thess. 3:3)

Reckon on God's Faithfulness to Guard your Future

By the way in which God establishes and guards the ones He has called to know Him and serve Him from the evil one, you can see that their assurance and hope of victory is rooted in His faithfulness, as this precious verse declares: verses in their own efforts "And I give unto them eternal life; and they shall never perish, neither shall any man pluck them out of My hand. My Father, which gave them to me, is greater than all; and no man is able to pluck them out of my Father's hand." (John 10:28, 29)

Reckon on God's Faithfulness to Draw Backsliders Back to Him

By the fact that He chastens His children when they go astray, the Believer discovers the faithfulness of God:
- "For whom the Lord loves He chastens, and scourges every son whom He receives" (Heb. 12:6).
- "If we confess our sins, He is faithful and just to forgive us our sins, and to cleanse us from all unrighteousness." (I John 1:9)

Reckon on God's Faithfulness to Forgive the Sins you Confess

What a promise to support this wonderful thing to reckon on: "If we confess our sins, He is faithful and just to forgive us our sins, and to cleanse us from all unrighteousness." (I John 1:9). Can you imagine what it will do for your soul to be able to trust the truth of this verse by reckoning on His promise to do what He says—even when you feel so unworthy of forgiveness (and may be reluctant to forgive yourself).

The key to confidence is to realize the powerful truths imbedded in this verse: (i) He is righteous, and (ii) He is faithful. This being the case, then, it would be wrong to doubt that your sin is forgiven when you have confessed it because it would reflect the fact that you are questioning His righteousness and His faithfulness.

A pastor tells the story of meeting a man who claimed that every night, just before he drifted off into sleep, he would confess all the sins he could remember, in case he should die in his sleep. When questioned as to why he did this he replied, "So that, in case, I die, I will be sure of going to God".

"But", answered the Pastor, "Isn't that a terrible slur on God's faithfulness? Did He not say, 'I will remember their sins no more'? Then the Pastor had the privilege of assuring this man that if he confessed his sin, God was faithful and just to forgive it, and to cleanse it away forever!

Reckon on God's Faithfulness to Answer Your Prayer of Faith

By the way in which He answers the prayers of His children. The Bible reveals that the righteousness, mercy and faithfulness of God run along nearly parallel lines, and they are all pledged to the deliverance, defense, and complete and eternal salvation of God's people.

Prayer is a true partnership with God. Your part is first to thoughtfully, deliberately, and believingly hand the matter over to Him. Then, second, dare to believe that He has taken it in hand and that, though He may keep you waiting, He will not rest until He has finished the matter.

Just think about the unique power you wield in praying a prayer of faith—your faith will actually set in motion the fullness of the omnipotent God, the ascended Christ.

As a pastor, I have found that true prayer has only two characteristics First, I must allow the Holy Spirit to winnow away what is inconsistent with God's will to grant, i.e., not to impose our will on Him, but allow Him to resolve the problems laid before his throne.

Second, I must cease worrying no matter how long the delay seems, nor however strong the combination of adverse circumstances. I must quiet my heart and exercise unwavering faith that my Lord will not rest until He has finished the matter that I laid before Him. In this way I am reckoning on His faithfulness.

Joshua's Last Word on Faithfulness

Is there any more important truth to embrace to strengthen your faith? Joshua would agree that the faithfulness of God is of singular importance.

In his final message to all of the assembled people he had led for so many years, as an associate to Moses, and then as their Commander, he offers them a single spiritual truth to provide them maximum support as they carry on without him: the faithfulness of God. Permit me to set the scene and tell you this magnificent story.

In Joshua 23, his "swan's song", Joshua makes a public address sharing his reflections on their incredible journey from Egypt into Canaan. He will later use it all to lead up to a serious warning. On this occasion, Joshua summons all of Israel before him to hear a reflection of their historic past, which he would afterwards use to lead up to a solemn warning. What stood out in his thinking? His mind was drawn to the faithfulness of God. It explained every good thing that had happened to them, "You know with all your heart and soul that not one of all the good promises the LORD your God gave you has failed. Every promise has been fulfilled; not one has failed" (23:14).

Then, Joshua warns the people now enjoying the Promised Land, "But just as every good promise of the LORD your God has come true, so the LORD will bring on you all the evil he has threatened, until he has destroyed you from this good land he has given you. (Josh. 23:15, 16).

Ah, that is the other side of God's faithfulness to His Word, isn't it? We warmly embrace the promises. But there is all the unsettling group of threats. And the same faithfulness that will move Him to meet His promises is the same attribute that ensures that He will fulfill all of His threats if we turn from trusting Him. The reason is simple: He cannot deny Himself.

All this boils down to the fact that the unchanging God is faithful at all times, not only to carry out His wonderful promises of blessings, but also His most solemn warnings and threats. God will remain faithful to both for He cannot disown Himself.

In spite of His faithfulness to us, we should be more concerned with our faithfulness to Him! This is the real issue that many fail to see. Before our earthly life is over, we may have to choose to die for Him or renounce our faith in Christ. If it comes to this, may we all remain faithful to Jesus as we bear in mind His eternal words:

"I tell you, my friends, do not be afraid of those who kill the body and after that can do no more. But I will show you whom you should fear: Fear him who, after the killing of the body, has power to throw you into hell. Yes, I tell you, fear him" (Luke 12:4,5).

Secret to Mountain Moving Faith: God's Faithfulness

Certainly all of these verses and comments are instructive, but nothing clarifies like some beautiful, real life examples of people reckoning on God's faithfulness. I share only three; but they are exemplary.

People Who Knew of God's Faithfulness

As you meditate on these think on these people, from the pages of the Scripture who beautifully exemplified these areas of God's faithfulness.

Samuel's Mother (I Sam. 1:18)

This woman was facing the worst calamity that could befall a Hebrew wife—she remained childless. We then observe her in the Temple praying with such fervor for God to open her womb that the High Priest thought she was drunk. Yet, shortly thereafter, when she joined her husband to partake of the sacrificial feast, "her face was no longer sad". What explains such a transformation?

As she wrestled in prayer, Eli, the High Priest came to her, and after discussion assured her that God had heard her prayer, and that she would bear a son. The wonderful look on her face was due to her trust in the promises spoken to her and behind them, her realization of the faithfulness of God. Reckoning on the faithfulness of God to answer her prayer, she sat down to the table with a solid confidence that a son would soon be born to her.

Nobleman's Son (John 4:50)

In the record of John's Gospel, we meet a man of unusual character, and thrust into the midst of one of the worst things a parent can face—the impending death of a young son.

This man of character suddenly remembers that nearby is Jesus; and stories abound that the man can heal the sick, among many other miracles. In desperation the man jumps up from the bedside of his dying son to seek help from the Savior.

Straightway he ran to meet Jesus. He shared his broken heart and his need. Then he heard the most precious words from the Savior, "Thy Son will live".

Can you imagine how quickly he made it back home? The reason is simple: upon hearing the words of the Master, he realized they were from the lips of One who is totally trustworthy. He received the promise of Jesus as a promise as good as gold. His pure trust in the trustworthiness of Jesus is confirmed. When he walked through the front door he was told, the healing was complete and instantaneous—and it occurred yesterday (the very hour when he spoke personally with the Lord.

Since the trip was not a two day journey, I am convinced that the man left Jesus with such confidence in the faithfulness of His promise that the man, exhausted from days of worry, stopped to get himself a good night's rest. Oh he blessed relief when you reckon on the faithfulness of God's promises! I imagine that had we been there we would have observed by watching him receive this report that his reaction reflected a lack of surprise.

The reason, if true, would be simple: he reckoned on God's word regarding his son's condition being faithful and true, and this assurance had produced within his soul the peace of God (Phil. 4:19).

Apostle Paul Shipwrecked (Acts 27:25, and 34)

Paul was on a ship bound for Rome to be put on trial for his life. During the voyage, a storm threatened to capsize the vessel and smash it to pieces. Everyone fell into a hysterical panic. But Paul rose to encourage everyone that they should not panic. He promised them that God had told him the ship's crew and passengers would all be spared. He then urged them to sit down and eat a hearty meal, since they may not get a next one for quite a while, and then abandon ship and head toward a nearby beach.

What was behind this man's counsel? I submit that it was complete confidence in the faithfulness of God's revelation to him. With safety assured, he lost all fear and found his appetite. What a picture of a man reckoning on God's faithfulness.

Ruth and Naomi's Second Chance

Such admirable women! Weary and penniless, yet steadfast in their love for each other and the God of Israel, these two widows arrive at Mother Naomi's hometown, Bethlehem. It had been years since Naomi lived there; for decades she lived and raised a family in a foreign country hundreds of miles away.

Naomi consulted the Lord and received a plan. She then instructed here daughter-in-law to go into the fields of her kinsman, Boaz, and work for him and, in the process, attempt to find favor with him.

In good time the promise seemed to be coming true. Ruth was given a job by Boaz, and then she did get close to him, and she did find favor with him. But he had to fulfill a responsibility as a kinsman redeemer to earn the right to ask Ruth to marry him. By God's faithful providence it all worked out.

I love the scene when Ruth has explained that Boaz has shared his love for her and pledged to seek with all his heart to secure the right to marry her. As she told all this to Naomi she began to pace the floor.

Finally Naomi could take this nervous movement no longer and exclaimed, "Sit still! My daughter, sit still!

I hear those words in my own soul, when I linger between a sure word of promise spoken to me by the Spirit through the Word and a haunting shadow of doubt. Then I hear the precious Lord, by the Holy Sprit say to me, "Sit still! Rest in Me and My Word and wait patiently for Me to fulfill it all for you" Do you not love it when you experience the precious Spirit telling you to relax and reckon on the faithfulness of Him by trusting in the faithfulness of His promises.

I hear you saying, now that my understanding of the faithfulness is great, I find myself more eager to know all the areas in which God declares Himself faithful. To this end, I have compiled seven areas. These promises are drawn from the hundreds that lay like diamonds in the truth of every page. As you meditate upon them, I pray that one or several will strike you as a nugget of gold you can capture to renew and refresh your faith, or hope or peace, as they have countless millions of dear believing Christians since He ascended to get into position to execute them in the fullness of His power for your benefit.

The Faithfulness of God

The faithfulness of God to the believer is expressed in many ways in the Bible including these:
1. The faithfulness of God to forgive sin.
   "If we confess our sin, He is faithful and just to forgive us our sin, and to cleanse us from all unrighteousness." (1 John 1:9).
2. The faithfulness of God in keeping us saved. Here I share two verses:
   - "If we believe not, yet He abides faithful; He cannot deny Himself." (2 Tim. 2:13);
   - "But the Lord is faithful who shall establish you and keep you from evil." (2 Thess. 3:3)
3. The faithfulness of God in times of pressure.
   "There has no testing taken you but such as is common to man; but God is faithful, who will not allow you to be tested above that you are able; but will with the testing also make a way to escape, that you may be able to bear it." (I Cor. 10:13)
4. The faithfulness of God in providing for us under the partnership of Christ.
   "God is faithful, by whom you were called into the fellowship of His Son, Jesus Christ." (I Cor. 1:9)
5. The faithfulness of God in keeping His promises to us.,
   "Let us hold fast the profession of our faith without wavering; for He is faithful that promised." (Heb. 10:23)
6. The faithfulness of God to us in times of suffering.
   "Wherefore let them that suffer according to the will of God commit the keeping of their souls to Him in well doing, as unto a faithful creator." (1 Pet. 4:19),
7. The faithfulness of God in providing for the believer's eternal future.
   "Faithful is He that calls you who also will do it!" (1 Thess. 5:24),

I challenge you to search each of these Bible verses. Consider this your homework!

Conclusion

As I close this final chapter, enjoy this amazing testimony of the faithfulness of God.

Roger Simms, hitchhiking his way home, would never forget the date--May 7.

His heavy suitcase made Roger tired. He was anxious to take off his army uniform once and for all. Flashing the hitchhiking sign (right fist closed, thumb extended) to the oncoming car, he lost hope when he saw it was a black, sleek, new Cadillac.

To his surprise the car stopped. The passenger door opened. He ran toward the car, tossed his suitcase in the back, and thanked the handsome, well-dressed man as he slid into the front seat. "Going home for keeps?" "Sure am," Roger responded. "Well, you're in luck if you're going to Chicago." "Not quite that far. Do you live in Chicago?" "I have a business there. My name is Hanover."

After talking about many things, Roger, a Christian, felt a compulsion to witness to this fifty-ish, apparently successful businessman about Christ. But he kept putting it off, till he realized he was just thirty minutes from his home. It was now or never. So, Roger cleared his throat, "Mr. Hanover, I would like to talk to you about something very important." He then proceeded to explain the way of salvation, ultimately asking Mr. Hanover if he would like to receive Christ as his Savior. To Roger's astonishment the Cadillac pulled over to the side of the road. Roger thought he was going to be ejected from the car. But the businessman bowed his head and received Christ, then thanked Roger. "This is the greatest thing that has ever happened to me."

Five years went by, Roger married, had a two-year-old boy, and a business of his own. Packing his suitcase for a business trip to Chicago, he found the small, white business card Hanover had given him five years before and decided that when he arrived in Chicago he would look up Hanover Enterprises.

When he arrived at the offices, a receptionist told him it was impossible to see Mr. Hanover, but he could see Mrs. Hanover. A little confused as to what was going on, he was ushered into a lovely office and found himself facing a keen-eyed woman in her fifties. She extended her hand. "You knew my husband?" Roger told how her husband had given him a ride when hitchhiking home after the war. "Can you tell me when that was?" "It was May 7, five years ago, the day I was discharged from the army."

Roger then asked her, "Excuse me M'am, but is there anything special about that day?" She was silent.

Roger then pondered if he should mention giving his witness? Since he had come so far, he figured that he might as well take the plunge.

"Mrs. Hanover, I explained the gospel to your husband. He then pulled over to the side of the road and wept against the steering wheel. He gave his life to Christ that day."

Explosive sobs shook her body. Getting a grip on herself, she sobbed, "I had prayed for my husband's salvation for years. I believed God would save him." Roger looked puzzled.

"And," said Roger, "Where is your husband now, Mrs. Hanover?"

She looked him in the eye and after a moment of silence said, "He's dead," Then she began to weep, struggling with words. "He was in a car crash after he let you out of the car. He never got home. You see--I thought God had not kept His promise."

Sobbing uncontrollably, she added, "I stopped living for God five years ago because I thought He had not kept His word!"

Well, dear reader, I will leave the rest to your imagination to piece together the ending of this story—how this woman returned to faith, simply by discovering, afresh, the absolute faithfulness of God.

I feel so sad for those who do not want a father in heaven so much as a grandfather in heaven; a senile benevolence who, as they say, "liked to see young people enjoying themselves" and whose plan for the universe was simply that it might be truly said at the end of each day, "a good time was had by all.

Truly, in the character of the living God, whose true character, including His faithfulness, becomes the source of our faith. We trust Him because we know He is completely trustworthy.

The challenge now comes to our generation. God has issued the call for men and women to invade cities and nations with the power of heaven. Will you answer the call of God? Will you dare to only believe? Is your heart so moved by compassion for the multitudes that will take God at His Word and step out?

Let it be said of our generation, "through faith (they) subdued Kingdoms, wrought righteousness, obtained promises, stopped the mouths

Secret to Mountain Moving Faith: God's Faithfulness

of lions, quenched the violence of fire, escaped the edge of the sword, out of weakness were made strong, waxed valiant in fight, turned to flight the armies of the aliens," (Heb. 11:33-34). Faith in God can move any mountain and will pull down any stronghold.

Stir up the gift of faith within you, and invade your home, your community, and your nation with the power of God. Let the will of God be done on earth through you—begin now to seek to live by the kind of faith

that can move a mountain and smash any stronghold.

God bless you as you learn to trust Him more and more!
Pastor Russell Ellies, D.Min.

www.ingramcontent.com/pod-product-compliance
Lightning Source LLC
Chambersburg PA
CBHW051932160426
43198CB00012B/2124